ALSO BY ALEC WILKINSON

The Happiest Man in the World (2007)

Mr. Apology (2003)

My Mentor (2002)

A Violent Act (1993)

The Riverkeeper (1991)

Big Sugar (1989)

Moonshine (1985)

Midnights (1982)

The Protest Singer

The Protest Singer

An Intimate Portrait of Pete Seeger

Alec Wilkinson

ALFRED A. KNOPF · *New York* · 2009

This Is a Borzoi Book Published by Alfred A. Knopf

Copyright © 2009 by Alec Wilkinson

All rights reserved. Published in the United States by
Alfred A. Knopf, a division of Random House, Inc., New York,
and in Canada by Random House of Canada, Limited, Toronto.
www.aaknopf.com

Knopf, Borzoi Books, and the colophon are registered trademarks
of Random House, Inc.

A portion of this work originally appeared in slightly different
form in The New Yorker.

Grateful acknowledgment is made to Ry Cooder for permission
to reprint an excerpt from "Three Chords and the Truth" by
Ry Cooder. Reprinted by permission of Ry Cooder.

Library of Congress Cataloging-in-Publication Data
Wilkinson, Alec, [date]
The protest singer : an intimate portrait of Pete Seeger /
by Alec Wilkinson. — 1st ed.

p. cm.

ISBN 978-0-307-26995-9

1. Seeger, Pete, 1919– 2. Folk singers—United States—
Biography. I. Title.
ML420.S445W55 2009
782.42162'130092—dc22
[B]   2008054387

Manufactured in the United States of America
First Edition

FOR
TIM DICKEY

Now they took Pete Seeger before the law,
put him on the witness stand,
but he stood right up to tyranny
with just a banjo in his hand.

Such a righteous banjo picker,
watching out for me and you,
that was just a man that wouldn't back down
on three chords and the truth.

Three chords and the truth,
three chords and the truth,
the only crime Pete Seeger done
was three chords and the truth.

He sang his freedom songs real good,
he's still getting his message through,
you better check out old Pete Seeger on
three chords and the truth.

—from "Three Chords and the Truth,"
Ry Cooder

The Protest Singer

IT WAS THE AMBITION of the singer and song-writer Pete Seeger as a child, in the 1920s, to be an Indian, a farmer, a forest ranger, or possibly an artist, because he liked to draw. He went to Harvard, joined the tenor banjo society, and studied sociology in the hope of becoming a journalist, but at the end of his second year he left before taking his exams and rode a bicycle west, across New York State. If he encountered a group of people making music on a porch or around a fire, he added himself to it and requested that they teach him the songs. He was tall and thin and earnest and polite. To eat, he made watercolor sketches of a farm from the fields, then knocked on the farmhouse door and asked to trade the drawing for a meal.

In the late 1940s, Seeger belonged to a group called the Almanac Singers, which included Woody Guthrie. The name derived from there being in most working-class homes two books, a Bible and an almanac, one for this world and one for the next. The Almanac

Singers appeared mainly at strikes and at rallies supporting the rights of laborers. Seeger says that the band was "famous to readers of the *Daily Worker*," the newspaper of the Communist Party. The Almanac Singers broke up in 1942, after Seeger was drafted. Following the war, Seeger performed on his own, then became a member of the Weavers, whose version of "Goodnight, Irene," by Huddie Ledbetter, called Leadbelly, was, for thirteen weeks in 1950, the best-selling record in America. The Weavers quit playing in 1952, after an informant told the House Un-American Activities Committee that three of the four Weavers, including Seeger, were Communists. (Seeger knew students at Harvard who were Communists, and, idealistically, he became one for several years, too.) Following the informant's testimony, the Weavers found fewer and fewer places to work. Seeger and his wife, Toshi, decided that Seeger should sing for any audience that would have him. They printed a brochure and sent it to summer camps, colleges, schools, churches, and any other organizations that they thought might be sympathetic. Seeger began engaging in what he calls "guerilla cultural tactics." Arriving in a town he'd been hired to play in, he'd call the local radio station, where the disc jockey, remembering the Weavers, would usually invite him to talk on the air. Seeger would discuss his concert then play that night and be gone before anyone had time to object. In towns where his appearances were more widely publicized, he grew accustomed to walking past pickets holding signs saying "Moscow's Canary" and "Khrushchev's Songbird." In *How Can I Keep from Singing,* a biography of Seeger, David Dunaway writes that a poll conducted during the period by Harvard said that 52 percent of the American people thought that Communists should be put in jail.

In 1955, a promoter brought the Weavers back together for a concert at Carnegie Hall—he had told each of them that the others wanted to. The concert sold out, and they began performing again. Seeger left them in 1958. One of the songs from their catalog, "Pay Me My Money Down," the lament of an indignant longshoreman, appears on *We Shall Overcome/The Seeger Sessions,* a record made by Bruce Springsteen in 2006. The other twelve songs on the record are versions of songs that Seeger recorded and tended to sing on his own.

Springsteen began listening to Seeger in 1998, when he was asked to provide a song for a Seeger tribute record (*Where Have All The Flowers Gone,* Appleseed Recordings). To choose one, he "went to the record store and bought every Pete record they had," he told me. "I really immersed myself in them, and it was very transformative. I heard a hundred voices in those songs, and stories from across the span of American history—parlor music, church music, tavern music, street and gutter music—I felt the connection almost intuitively, and that certain things needed to be car-

ried on; I wanted to continue doing things that Pete
had passed down and put his hand on. He had a real
sense of the musician as historical entity—of being a
link in the thread of people who sing in others' voices
and carry the tradition forward—and of the song-
writer, in the daily history of the place he lived, that
songs were tools, and, without sounding *too* preten-
tious, righteous implements when connected to historical consciousness. At the same time, Pete always
maintained a tremendous sense of fun and lightness,
which is where his grace manifested itself. It was
cross-generational. He played for anyone who would
listen; he played a lot for kids. When I set the musicians up in my house to make this record, and we
started playing Pete's songs, my daughter said, 'That
sounds like fun, what is that?' "

The Seeger Sessions does not include any songs that
Seeger wrote—such as "Turn, Turn, Turn," which sold
nearly a million records for the Byrds, in 1965. Springsteen recorded "If I Had a Hammer," but felt that it
asserted itself too forcefully among the rest of the
songs, possibly because it was so well known. The
thirteen songs he chose, he said, are "ones that I heard
my own voice in. When you're going through material that way, you're always trying to find your place
in the story. That's your part in the passing down of
that music. You have to know what you're adding.
Every time a folk song gets sung, something gets
added to that song. Why did I pick Pete Seeger songs

instead of songs by the Carter Family or Johnny Cash or the Stanley Brothers? Because Pete's library is so vast that the whole history of the country is there. I didn't feel I had to go to someone else's records. It was very broad. He listened to everything and collected everything and transformed everything. Everything I wanted, I found there."

SEEGER FIGURED in the lives of my parents and older brothers, but I am not the right age to have been much aware of him at firsthand. I heard him sing only once. I remember standing one night in August with my brothers and my mother and father in a parking lot among people who towered over me, and waiting until a tall, thin man with a banjo came out the back door of the town hall in Wellfleet, Massachusetts, and sang several songs on a landing. I suppose I was five or six, meaning it would have been 1957 or 1958. Being among a crowd at night was a novelty for me, and because of that, and the close attention everyone paid, it was a dramatic occasion, but I don't remember the music. Only years later did I learn why Seeger meant so much to the people gathered to hear him, and how rare a person he is.

When someone lives a long time, his life achieves a discernible pattern, an almost topographical sort of map depicting his influences and their effects as they emerge, recede, combine in the shadows, and re-emerge. Some of Seeger's influences derive from the nineteenth-century and Calvinist habits of mind. Parts exemplify a line of New England thinking, descended from the New Testament through Emerson and Thoreau. Its hallmarks are a reverence for nature, a regard for human life, something like scorn for the nurturing of materialistic values, and a belief in the worth of right moral behavior. Seeger's faith in music as a means of achieving among groups of people feelings that can't be achieved on one's own came by way of the family line and his own emphatic experience.

What I had in mind when I called Seeger to ask if I might try writing about him was a small, descriptive book, a long essay—a factual novella, if that is the right term. I didn't know if he would consent to it. I thought he might turn me down flat. "Too much has been written about me, and at too great length," he said. I had stammered only four or five words in reply when he added, "What's needed is a book that can be read in one sitting."

SEEGER WAS BORN on May 3, 1919. He and Toshi, who is half Japanese, live in Beacon, New York, about sixty miles north of Manhattan. They were married in 1943. Their house is remote and surrounded by woods. Seeger chops wood every day and complains when he can't. (In Africa once, he bought an ax and carried it in his banjo case, and a man there told him it was the first time he had ever seen a white man use an ax.) Trying to recall a name or a fact, he sometimes places one hand over his forehead and closes his eyes. His conversation passes quickly from one subject to another, giving the impression that many things are occurring to him at once. When he speaks at any length, he tends to look into the middle distance, as if addressing an audience there. He is still tall and thin and remarkably lithe. To retrieve something from indoors if he is outside, or at some distance away, he often jogs off. He has a sharp nose and full, round cheeks, a high-colored complexion and teeth that lean slightly to one side, like an old fence. His eyes are blue and heavily lidded and so small that he seems to be

regarding a person from some remove. His gaze is sur-
prisingly fleeting and indirect for someone whose
manner is so straightforward. That he is more com-
fortable with ideas and enthusiasms than with inti-
macy is a judgment one often hears applied to him.

His tastes in reading favor anthropology, biography, and philosophy. In a corner of his living room is
a black and gold rocking chair from Harvard, and
above a couch is a map of the world. By the phone is
a little sign that says, "Please let me speak before you
hang up."

Seeger never aspired to a career as a singer, and he
dislikes being so well known. Celebrity, he thinks,
comes for most people at the expense of others whose
accomplishments tend to be more substantial. "I
never liked the music business and the kind of fame
you got," he says. "Agents are hired to get you publicity, when there are people in every community who
are extraordinary—a woman who might have raised
six children on her own and not a one of them ever
got into trouble, or someone who made one contribution or another to the quality of life in a small town—
and you never hear about them, but their neighbors
know who they are. Heroic people, and they never get
publicized. Maybe once, when they die. People wonder why such a big crowd turns out at their funerals,
but their neighbors know." He was pleased that Bruce
Springsteen, whom he regards as a friend, recorded
songs from his past—he thinks they are good songs,

and he is gratified by the thought that so many people would hear them—but the mail and the attention that followed were an encumbrance. He already received so many letters that he and Toshi were able to answer them only with postcards—and besides, he still has work he wants to do. His vitality sometimes seems boundless, and his nature is almost unflaggingly hopeful, but a line of melancholy runs through it. Once, after a performance in Spain that didn't go well, he wrote in a journal, "I seem to stagger about this agonized world as a clown, dressed in happiness, hoping to reach the hearts and minds of the young. When newspaper reporters ask me what effect my songs have, I try and make a brave reply, but I am really not so certain."

WHEN SEEGER WAS YOUNGER, his singing voice fell between the range of an alto and a tenor, what is called a split tenor. It was robust—it sounded like the voice that comes from a few rows behind you in church and that everyone follows—and even in complicated passages his pitch was precise. He had a dramatic falsetto which he could deliver as a moan or a shout. He sang without vibrato or with only an occasional trace of it. His phrasing was subtle but resourceful enough to inflect meaning and character and to enliven a narrative, but not so much as to divert the listener toward the singer's personality. His presence onstage was confident, offhand, and compelling, but he regarded any attention paid him as a performer to be misplaced. An implement for delivering a song is more how he saw himself.

He approached show business uneasily. His biographer, David Dunaway, describes a column Seeger published in *Sing Out,* a folk song quarterly, which he signed with Toshi's name, and in which he said that his catalog amounted to "one of the most uneven bodies of recorded music that any performer could boast of, or perhaps be ashamed of . . . If one could dub onto a tape a few songs from here and there on his many LPs, one might have quite a good one-hour tape of Pete Seeger. The trouble is, no two people would make the same selections. Therein lies his defense." Dunaway writes that Seeger was so uncomfortable with being an entertainer that he sometimes urged people not to buy his records. He preferred that they sing the songs themselves.

Seeger believes that songs can make someone feel powerful when he isn't by any measure except his own determination. He embraced as a young man the conviction that songs are a way of binding people to a cause. A piece of writing might be read once or twice, he says, a song is sung over and over. Every word in every song he ever sang was intelligible, which had a lot to do with the force of his performances. The issue at stake, he says, between him and Bob Dylan at the Newport Folk Festival, in 1965, when he said that he wished he had an ax to cut the cable supplying electricity to the stage, was not that Dylan had performed with electric instruments—Howlin' Wolf had done that the day before, he points out, there were no prohibitions against it—but that no one could hear the words to Dylan's song. "It was a good song, too," Seeger told me. " 'Maggie's Farm.' " He was sure that Dylan wanted the audience to hear the words—else why sing the song?—and that the people in charge of the microphones were sabotaging him.

When he was nineteen, in 1938, his stepmother, a

musician, told him, "Peter, you have a talent for song leading. I think you should develop it." Having people sing with him was not merely a means of gratifying an audience's desire to be entertained, as the practice became with singers who imitated him (which is why it also became weary and insincere and so easily caricatured). He hoped that by making people feel themselves to be elements of a collective identity, he could intensify their experience—enlarge and encourage them and help hold oblivion at arm's length. People who sang in church and in pursuit of mystical states of being knew this, people who sang in the fields knew this, people who sang hymns and anthems to prepare for war had always known it. Seeger had been schooled to employ singing it as a method for social change. Martin Luther King inspired people to seek just treatment. In King's wake, Seeger emboldened them to pursue it. During the most fractious periods of discourse in the 1960s, Seeger's earnest and unadorned desire to unite disparate people had a pacifying effect. It smoothed the rougher edges of the hectoring. A song when he sang it and a crowd sang with him was a version of worldly benediction.

Seeger has always preferred to hear his voice among other voices, rather than alone (folk songs sound better, he thinks, when sung by a crowd). More than once, he tried to start a chorus. The first time was after World War II. The last time was in New York City during the late 1980s. He had hoped that

after the chorus was sufficiently rehearsed it would sing on the streets, but it attracted a certain number of people who couldn't sing at all. His belief in a chorus as a democratic body meant that he couldn't ask them to leave, but their presence discouraged people who could actually sing. "It wasn't a chorus as a chorus should be," he says. "The best people left, and the worst ones stayed," and he gave it up as unworkable. He regards its failure as personal.

As for his effect on audiences, this story was told to me by a man named John Cronin, who has known Seeger for thirty-five years. "I teach a course at Pace

University called 'Citizen Advocacy in the Evolution of American Democracy,' " he said. "Freshmen and sophomores, mostly eighteen and nineteen. I thought, I'm going to ask Pete to meet the class, because he can talk about the movements we're going to cover—labor, civil rights, the peace movement, the environmental movement. He's supported advocacy, he's changed democracy. He's a walking history of the role of the citizen.

"The day arrives. 2001. I say, 'We have a real treat coming up. Pete Seeger is going to join us.' And I can tell that I'm talking to an oil painting. They don't know who he is. One kid who's a little older thinks that he might be the father of Bob Seger of the Silver Bullet Band, and the other kids, who are younger, are going, 'What's the Silver Bullet Band?' Pete walks in with his banjo. He's eighty-two. We get a lot of hip-hop and streetsmart kids, they are a hard group to impress; he's playing to them cold. They didn't care about his past; there was more than sixty years between them. He's not an icon to them. They look at him and say, 'What is this?' He doesn't mind. Within five minutes, he has them singing the union song 'I Dreamed I Saw Joe Hill Last Night.' And at the next class they talked about him for forty-five minutes."

Folk songs frequently contain every kind of trouble and harm. Often they are songs that people sung to themselves or with their neighbors to commemorate a disaster or to give themselves courage or to console

themselves for losses and defeats and suffering and hardship. Sometimes they celebrate victories, but typically there is more misfortune than triumph. Folk songs have a lot of dark corners. They don't muse so much. They don't describe life from a balcony overlooking a harbor from which the boat is departing at sunset with your sweetheart. The folk song version of

that is We-were-to-wed, but-I-killed-her-instead. A lot of folk songs are about shipwrecks and strikes and mine collapses and heroes dying by the hands of cowards. They can go on and on. Dylan's recordings of songs that were ten minutes long, verse upon verse, were radical in the context of rock and roll, but he was making use of a conventional folk music form. It is no observation of my own that Seeger did more to make people aware of folk music in the middle of the twentieth century than any other performer. Not that everyone thanked him for it. David Dunaway writes that purists often resented Seeger's influence. Folk songs, they believed, were the product of refinements made by different singers in different places. They were a species of dialect. A true folksinger knew not only the way a song was sung in Kentucky, but also its variations in Oklahoma and Tennessee, not to mention its antecedents from Wales. Once Seeger recorded a song, they said, his version became so widely known that it effaced the others.

SEEGER BOUGHT HIS LAND in Beacon in 1949. He and Toshi had two small children, they were living in Greenwich Village, in a brownstone, with Toshi's parents, and they wanted to move to the country. Seeger was thirty, and Toshi was twenty-seven.

He was becoming well known as a musician, but they had no money yet to speak of. A real estate agent showed them properties he regarded as inexpensive. "I remember a big barn at one place and a little stream and some woods," Seeger told me one day. "Five thousand dollars. I said, no, I couldn't afford it." The agent showed them an old barn with some land for three thousand dollars. "I said I couldn't afford that, either." The agent asked, "What can you afford?" Seeger said, "How about just some land." He showed them a patch of woods on the side of a mountain set back from the river.

It had been part of a woodlot attached to one of the brickyards that used to operate along the riverbank. "Handmade bricks," Seeger said. "All the yards had mountain land above them. They'd carry the wood to the river on a sledge and turn it into charcoal and bricks. The whole mountain had been clear-cut, in

1911, except this parcel. It had a cliff, and no one wanted to climb it. They thought it was too steep to build on, but I climbed up here and saw that it leveled off at the top for a bit, and there was room to put a house."

Seeger brought Toshi to the top of the cliff and said, "See what a nice view we'll have." Toshi is small and dark-haired and more practical than Seeger. She looked around at the brush and the trees that enclosed them and said, "View of what?" From one of his brothers, Seeger borrowed a hundred dollars. His mother lent him three hundred. He and Toshi paid $1,750 for seventeen and a half acres. That summer they moved to the property with their children, a girl and a boy who were one and three (later they had another daughter), and lived in a twelve-foot trailer while Seeger chopped down trees. A stream ran through a ravine below their campsite. Toshi would strap her younger child to her hip and have the older one grab her skirt, and they would go down to the stream like pioneers and collect water for cooking and washing. Seeger was often gone on the weekends, working. At the end of August, he was to sing in Peekskill, a few miles away, on a stage in a field at a concert to benefit the Harlem chapter of the Civil Rights Congress. The star of the concert was Paul Robeson, whose father had been a slave. Robeson had a law degree from Columbia, but he made his living as an actor and singer. He had played Othello in London and on Broadway, and he had appeared in London in the stage version of *Show Boat,* and later in the movie. In 1934 he had gone to Russia and become persuaded that Russian society was more just than America's was, and he became a Communist. The Peekskill paper wrote that he was "violently and loudly pro-Russian."

The Ku Klux Klan had a chapter in Peekskill. Before the concert, vigilantes tore down the stage. The sponsors built another stage, and the concert was rescheduled for September 4. Dunaway writes that during the interval, the Ku Klux Klan sent a letter to an organization that Seeger had been part of, People's Artists, thanking it and Seeger for the 722 applications for membership it had received since the stage had been destroyed.

Seeger and Toshi, their children, Toshi's father, and two friends of the Seegers drove to Peekskill for the concert. A lot of people arrived from Harlem in chartered buses. They passed men and women and children who shouted obscenities at them. There were woods on three sides of the field where the stage was and a road on the fourth. Members of several unions surrounded the field so that no one could get into the concert without a ticket, a means, they hoped, of keeping the vigilantes out. A woman named Sylvia Koch sang the "Star-Spangled Banner." "A pianist named Leonid Hambro played Prokofiev," Seeger said, "I played two or three songs—a country blues I learned from Woody Guthrie called 'T for Texas, T for Tennessee,' and I sang 'If I Had a Hammer,' for one of the first times.

"Paul Robeson sang 'Old Man River,' from *Show Boat,* which he was famous for. Men stood behind him and on either side, so that he wouldn't be hit by a sniper firing from the woods. I suppose they could have got him from the woods in front, behind the audience, but you couldn't have someone stand in front of him while he sang."

The concert ended in the afternoon—the organizers wanted everyone to be able to leave before dark. Robeson got into a car then out the other side of it and into another and possibly into a third one.

"Unless you were watching closely, you wouldn't have known what car he was in," Seeger said. Robeson's car was among the first to leave. Seeger left about an hour after the concert ended. When he tried to make the turn toward Beacon, a policeman diverted him. All the traffic was made to travel on the same winding road. On the road were pieces of glass. "Around a corner was a young man throwing stones at each car that passed," Seeger said. "The cars were moving slowly, and he'd run right up beside them and launch the stones from four feet as hard as he could. They were about the size of a baseball. They came from piles of them that were built up beside the road.

While we were singing, they had been collecting stones."

Toshi's father put the children on the floor of the car and lay on top of them. Rocks broke all the windows except the back one. Seeger saw a policeman farther up the road. "I stopped and shouted, 'Officer, aren't you going to do something?' All he said was, 'Move on. Move on.' " Seeger realized that because he had paused, the man behind him was being set upon, so he drove ahead. When the chartered buses reached Harlem that evening, riders told a reporter from the *New York Times* that all the way to Yonkers, nearly twenty-five miles, people had thrown stones at them.

Seeger drove to a campground that had showers—there was no running water at his place—and he and Toshi and her father washed the glass from the children's hair. They all had to move carefully so as not to be cut by shards that were hidden in their clothes.

AFTER SEEGER HAD CLEARED two acres, he went to the New York Public Library, on Forty-second Street, and looked up "log cabin." Like Thoreau, he planned to build a house from trees he had cut down. Thoreau's cabin was a single room for a man who lived alone. Seeger's cabin needed to accommodate a family. The Weavers were beginning to work in nightclubs in the city. Seeger would either take an evening train to join them, or he would drive. If he drove, he'd make his way early in the morning up the West Side of Manhattan, between Fourteenth and Thirty-fourth Streets, and when he found a packing crate thrown out on the sidewalk, he would knock it apart with a hammer and take the wood home. Much of it he used for the roof. (For some time, until he painted the ceiling, you could read on it stenciled phrases such as "Made in Occupied China," or "Military Government of Italy.") If he didn't drive, he would catch the night train delivering mail up the Hudson. The train stopped at each town. Seeger would sleep on the train and arrive home to have breakfast with his family.

People would visit from the city and Seeger would hand them a shovel or a pair of clippers. The trees he had cut down for the house were still in the woods. "I had to go as much as two hundred feet from the house to find enough straight ones," he said. At the end of three months he had seventy logs. With the help of friends he had intended to haul the logs to where he had dug the foundation, "but I got fifteen people here and found they couldn't lift one log."

Instead, he found a man in Beacon with a draft horse. "His name was Walter Shannon," Seeger said. "I can still see the roof of his house from the lawn. He only died recently. How he got the draft horse here, I don't know. I guess he walked it. Anyway, he showed up in the morning, and he had a long chain. He walked up the hill with the horse, and he'd wrap the chain around the log and slap the horse, and then he

went running after it, wrapping the reins around tree trunks. He said once you got the horse started, you didn't want it to stop."

Seeger walked me through the cabin, which no one lives in presently—he and Toshi live in a larger house built later on the other side of a small clearing. Past the front door was a big room with tree-trunk beams, a stone fireplace, a raised platform with a stove and a sink, and a picture window. Through the window, below us, was the river, about a mile away. "That was our first extravagance," Seeger said of the window. "A hundred dollars. Plus I had three old, old windows I stole from the sidewalk—someone was tearing down a house where now they have the law school for NYU, at the south side of Washington Square. The windows and doors were being stacked outside to be burned up or thrown away. I arrived with my old jeep and took two doors and a whole batch of windows. It was 1951, the year after we built the house. Then we started earning money, the royalties from 'Goodnight, Irene' were coming in, and we could have a whole well done, which cost several hundred dollars." He stepped across the room and stood beside the picture window. "I'm a smash bang carpenter," he said. "I put up some shelves to hold records and books right here, and the baby's crib was under it. One night we heard a terrible crash, and the shelf and all the books and records had come down on her crib. Fortunately, it was a strong oak crib." He shook his head. "That's the kind of stupid thing I've done all my life," he said plaintively. "I have taken greater risks than I should have in raising my children. I remember walking along the edge of a cliff with my son and not watching him closely. Because I could watch myself, I took it for granted that he could." He shrugged. "Anyway, my daughter's fifty-eight now."

He said that the bulk of the wood in the house was

oak, but that he had also used maple and hickory. He hadn't expected ever to have enough money for electricity, so he made no allowance for the wires to enter the foundation. Three years later, to install them, he had to dig underneath it. Off the kitchen was a second room, where there was a bed and a rocking chair, some books, and another stone fireplace. "The first stonework was terrible," Seeger said, thrusting his chin toward the fireplace. "It didn't have any form or design. I made lots of mistakes—cement made anyone who wanted to be a mason. After that I went around sketching all the old farmhouses in Dutchess County for their stonework, and I learned that the old masons would set their best stones at the corners and run a line between them, then build up the courses."

Several inches above the fireplace were two stones that were smaller than the stones around them. One was about the size of a softball, and the other had paving tar around it and gravel embedded like shrapnel in the tar. "They came into the car during the riot and didn't go out," Seeger said. "I thought that if I put them there, I would never forget what had happened."

WE CLOSED THE DOOR on the cabin and walked over to the main house. Toshi was leaving to run errands in town. Everything we needed to make soup and salad for lunch was in the refrigerator, she said. She told Seeger that she was putting a pear tart in the toaster oven for dessert. "This is practice for Pete," she told me. "I want to be sure, in case I go join my ancestors, that he can take care of himself. I don't want to have to lower baskets of food from the heavens." Before she left, she took the phone off the hook. "It's been ringing all morning," she said.

We sat down to eat at a table by a window, with the river at our backs. Because I asked him to, Seeger talked about his background. "I come from a family of doctors and shopkeepers and intellectuals," he said. "A great-uncle, Franklin Edson, was mayor of New York. He was a well-to-do lawyer, and he came in as a kind of compromise candidate and served only one term. He christened the Brooklyn Bridge. Edson was almost like a father to my grandfather, because my great-grandfather had been killed. He ran a small factory in Troy, New York, making boilers for a brewery, and in 1855 his wife said, 'Please don't go to work today, I've dreamed something terrible is going to happen.' He said, 'Of course I have to go to work, I have things to do. I can't not go because you had a vision.' Around the middle of the morning she hears a boom, and an hour later workmen brought his hand to her door with his wedding ring on it, the only piece they could find. He'd been blown up testing a boiler. After that, the family thought she had second sight. Franklin, when he dedicated the Brooklyn Bridge, there had been a lot of speeches, and when his time came he said, 'Ladies and gentlemen, I think that everything that needs to be said has been said,' then he sat down to applause."

Seeger poured himself a glass of water. "One relative was headmaster of Dalton, a private school in Manhattan," he said. "Another of a school Teddy Roosevelt went to. His name was Elie Charlier, and he was my French great-grandfather, my mother's side. He was the son of a Huguenot minister in Lyon, the textile town in eastern France. He must have been a smart kid, because he got a scholarship to a good school in Switzerland, where he made a discovery: rich people pay a lot of money for their kids to go to

school, and he must have thought, Why don't I run a school? Where? Paris? Too much competition. How about New York? So he saved his money and got passage to the city. He printed up a brochure on very fine paper saying, 'Ladies and gentlemen, if you want your sons to enter the diplomatic service, they must speak French. Send him to study with Elie Charlier,' and he rented a room in a posh district, and was a good teacher, and pretty soon he had hired other teachers, and he had an actual school, the Charlier Institute. This was around 1850. Eventually it was New York's leading preparatory school, mostly for children from

New York families, but he had the top floor as a dormitory for students from other parts of the country. It was on Fifty-eighth Street, between Fifth and Sixth—a big brownstone six stories high and sixty feet wide. My mother took me to see it just before it was torn down to make way for the Barbizon Plaza Hotel. Just a couple of years ago, I came across a little pamphlet printed in 1880, when the new building had been finished. It's an elegant little pamphlet describing the location of the new building—before that I think it had been down in Gramercy Park. He names on two pages the families who had sent their children there: the Astors, the Roosevelts, and Hamilton Fish, from the prominent Hudson River family."

A cat jumped onto the table and lay down on some letters. "Seeger is a German name," he went on. "My great-great-grandfather, Carl Ludwig Seeger, was being trained as a veterinarian, in the service of a duke. When he had the opportunity, though, he gave the duke the slip and left a note saying that he preferred to be a doctor of people. He had read the Declaration of Independence and was determined to come to this country. I see him standing on a dock and showing his diploma to a sea captain and saying, 'Wouldn't you like a doctor on your ship?' He went first to Charleston, South Carolina, and found that in spite of the Declaration of Independence there was slavery. He stayed six or seven years, married, and came up to Northampton, Massachusetts. In those days, child-

hood diseases swept away children. Only three boys of his thirteen children lived to be adults."

Seeger said that his paternal grandfather had made money in refining sugar in Mexico and had an estate with servants on Staten Island, where his father grew up, but by that time the family was living on its capital. Then the conversation turned toward his father, Charles, who was also a musician, but a scholarly one. "My father was a big influence on me," Seeger said. Somewhat mournfully, he added, "He was over-enthusiastic all his life. First about this, then about that." Seeger's older brother, John, once told an interviewer, "The biggest danger for Peter was whether he'd be swallowed up in Father's dreams."

CHARLES WAS BORN in 1886, in Mexico City. As a teenager he became an expert pianist. He liked to go to symphony concerts, and he could look at complicated scores and know what the music should sound like. "He thought the great symphonies would save the human race," Seeger said. "He thought they had something to teach us that couldn't be expressed in words." He went to Harvard, "where he did well in music but not so well in everything else," and then he went to Germany to do graduate work, intending to become a conductor or the director of a symphony. As a guest conductor at the Cologne Opera, he realized that he couldn't hear the flutes—"they were lost to him," Seeger said—and that he was going deaf. Following Beethoven's example, he decided to become a composer. Having returned to New York, he met Constance de Clyvver Edson, the mayor's grandniece, and a violinist. The two of them played duets at society parties, "a soiree here, a soiree there," Seeger said. Because it was customary in society that women should not appear among people they hadn't been introduced to, they sometimes played behind a screen. In 1911, they were married.

In photographs taken when Constance was young, she has dark hair, a full mouth, broad cheekbones, a

round face, and widely set eyes—Seeger's daughter Tinya resembles her. She had been raised in Paris and Tunisia. Her father was John Tracy Edson, the mayor's son, and a doctor. "I met him only once, when I was seven," Seeger said. "He was living at Sailor's Snug Harbor, a dreary little place on Staten Island, full of old sailors. His wife didn't want to see him again. He qualified for life in a sailor's home because he had gone to Annapolis. When he was seventeen, he had told his mother that he wanted to enroll there, but the congressmen and senators had already made their appointments"—candidates at the military colleges have to be proposed by members of Congress—"but President Grant hadn't yet made his. This was 1877, so he and his mother went to Washington from New York and hired a carriage at the train station, and while his mother waited in the carriage outside the White House, he went in and had an interview with the president and whether he got accepted then or heard later by telegram, he ended up at Annapolis. He served as an ensign, the lowest rank, in the Spanish-American War, and was in the harbor at Havana when a Spanish ship sank, and the Spanish sailors were swimming for their lives, and my grandfather said to his captain, 'I know how to handle small boats, I'm a yachtsman.' He took a lifeboat and rescued some of them. He died at seventy-nine, living in that little room about eight feet square. Being a doctor, he knew what pills to take."

Constance was also born in 1886, in Denver, where her parents had moved from New York, because her mother kept spending money her husband didn't have. " 'Darling, you bought these silk curtains, we can't afford them,' " Seeger said his grandfather would say, and she would answer, " 'You're a doctor, go and earn the money.' I suppose he wasn't a very good doctor," Seeger said. "She was a virago, a woman you can't manage, who does what she wants to do." By what means she met and fell in love with a member of the French diplomatic consulate, Seeger isn't sure, but she left her husband and took Seeger's mother and followed the man to Paris. Her husband followed, too. Only Seeger's mother was at their hotel when he arrived. "He was drinking and ripping off his clothes and storming around the room saying, 'When

that woman comes back, I'm going to kill her,' "
Seeger said. "My thirteen-year-old mother had to get a
message to her mother, saying, 'Do not come back to
the hotel until Father is no longer here.' Somehow she
did it."

Constance auditioned for a place at a conservatory
in Paris. She went to listen as the names of the pupils
were read and didn't hear hers and went back to the
hotel and told her mother she hadn't been accepted.
A messenger arrived to say that she had. She had listened for Edson the way her ear was accustomed to
hearing it in Colorado and had missed the French pro-
nunciation. From France, Constance and her mother
followed the Frenchman to a posting in Tunisia, where
they took rooms in a convent.

IN COLOGNE, Seeger's father had befriended a man
named Benjamin Wheeler, who became the president
of the University of California at Berkeley. Wheeler
was a classicist and wanted the university to have
an enviable musicology department, and he invited
Charles to run it. "So at age twenty-four, my father
was put in charge, and he got an unexpected education himself," Seeger said. "In sociology and history.
He was socialized when another professor took him to
the lettuce fields a hundred miles east of San Francisco, and he saw children the same age as me and my
brothers being worked to the bone. Later, he stood

and described this to an audience—'This is disgraceful that things like this go on in America, where whole families have their children laboring out there for pennies'—and a working-class voice sounded from the back of the hall, 'Shut up. You guys are just discovering this; we've known it all our lives.' "

When the United States entered World War I, in 1917, Charles made speeches denouncing the war as an imperialist one. His wife asked him not to— "She was afraid," Seeger said, "pacifists were being lynched"—but he persisted. His opinions caused some of his colleagues to spurn him. The newspapers ran photographs of Belgian babies being spitted by German soldiers. "My father remembered meeting a man on the campus who had been a friend and who now walked past him without a word," Seeger said. "My father asked what was the matter and the man said, 'I don't speak to people who approve of babies being bayoneted.' " Feeling against the Germans was so strong that restaurants sometimes changed the name of sauerkraut to Liberty Cabbage. Charles was asked to buy a war bond and refused. Under the pressure of his isolation, his health began to fail. According to Dunaway, he lost so much weight that his clothes hung on him. Even without his hearing problems, he was probably too scrawny to be a soldier, but as if to compound his troubles he insisted on registering for the draft as a conscientious objector.

"My grandfather and grandmother Seeger were

probably quite unhappy with my father's radicalism,"
Seeger said. "My grandfather was a Republican, and
my grandmother came from business people who
were good Republicans and Unitarians and very anti-
Semitic. When my older brother told them that he
had married, she said it was wonderful. 'You should
know my wife's Jewish,' he said, and she turned white
and said, 'You may never enter our door again.' Then
she left the room. My grandfather, I think, spoke to
her." Another impediment to Charles's position within
his family was that his younger brother, Alan, in order
to fight the Germans, had joined the French Foreign

Legion, in 1914, since the Americans weren't yet in the war. Alan had also gone to Harvard and then had lived for two years as a poet and playwright in New York before moving to Paris. In a photograph, wearing a pith helmet and with a mustache, and staring into the lens, he is the very model of a resolute Bohemian soldier. "Alan, you're a damn fool," Charles wrote him. "Don't you know the class of people that run France is the same class that runs Germany? You should have stayed out of it." One of Alan's poems, published in 1917, and called "Rendezvous," begins, "I have a rendezvous with death." He was killed by machine-gun fire on July 4, 1916, in a charge. It is said that after he fell, he cheered on his companions.

Charles wasn't drafted, but the university gave him a sabbatical, with the understanding that he wouldn't return. In something like an attitude of defeat, or at least of despair, he and his wife took their children back east on a train. "Somewhere on the way my father got this grand scheme," Seeger said. "He told my mother, 'Rather than save our music for the rich people in the city, why not take it out and play it for people in the small towns?' He was going to be a one-family chautauqua, bringing music to the workers."

CHARLES'S PARENTS, on property they owned in Patterson, New York, about sixty miles north of Manhattan, had a cow and horse barn, and in the winter of

1918 he began painstakingly building in it a trailer to haul behind his car. He used mostly maple, and tongue-and-groove construction, and it took a year and a half. Seeger turned in his chair and showed me on the wall, among a collection of family photographs, a small, shiny, black-and-white one depicting Charles and his wife, Pete as a baby, and his two older brothers, standing on the sidewalk in New York beside a black Model T Ford. Behind the car is a portion of what looks like a covered wagon. Beneath the trailer was a platform that slid out to support a folding organ, the kind that chaplains used in World War II. With the cover removed, the trailer became a stage, and at night the family slept on it. They left New York in January of 1921 and drove slowly south, stopping in small towns, and intending eventually to reach Florida. The novelty the family presented drew crowds that the music didn't hold. In Richmond, Virginia, the pavement was so hot that the tires sank into it. "The trip was a disaster," Seeger said. At night his mother did the family's laundry in a pot of water over a fire. The night she caught Peter, a year and a half old, about to step into the fire was the night she called it off.

The Seegers returned to Patterson. Years earlier, during Constance's childhood in Colorado, her mother, seeing that Constance had a talent for music, had taken her into a music store in Denver to ask what instrument might suit her. The young man who helped them was bright and engaging, and Constance's mother told him that he should be in New York, not wasting his time behind a counter in Colorado, and that if he were ever to go there, he must let her know, and she would arrange some introductions for him. About fifteen years later he arrived and started a school called the Institute of Musical Art, which became Juilliard. When Constance and Charles returned north, in 1923, they got jobs there; Charles taught musical theory, and Constance taught violin. Charles parked the trailer in the barn where he had built it, and it hardly ever moved again. The first summer they were home they also lived in the barn, then they moved to Nyack. Seeger said that he remembered

his father "running to catch the train as it left the station, jumping aboard, and turning to wave to me."

Seeger went to the first and second grade in Nyack, then his parents sent him to a boarding school in Ridgefield, Connecticut. All he remembers of it was drawing pictures of some of the other boys, and sitting astride a draft horse that had been brought to the school for the students to ride. He came home after eight months, when his father discovered that his son had caught scarlet fever, and no one at the school had told him.

The Protest Singer

. . .

SEEGER'S LIFE IN NYACK was solitary. His two brothers were sufficiently older to seem as if in another world. "I didn't have much family life," he said. His mother would leave instruments around the house for him to find, and by the time he was five or six, he could play songs on the organ, the marimba, and the piano. She wanted him trained as a classical musician, but he didn't care to be. She taught her students to remain still when they played, so that all their attention was directed toward the music, but Seeger couldn't keep from tapping his foot. When she tried to get him to learn to read music, he said that he just wanted to have fun; he thought that reading music was like painting by numbers. She worried that he would grow up to be a musical illiterate. "Years later I asked my father, 'When do you think people *should* learn to read music?' " Seeger said. "And he told me, 'When they know what kind of music they want to play.' He said, 'You don't learn to read before you speak, and you don't learn to dance before you walk.' " In addition, Seeger had a renegade streak, encouraged by the atmosphere of the household. His parents were friends with a modernist composer named Henry Cowell, and Seeger remembers when he was six seeing Cowell play the piano with his fists.

In the summer of 1927 Seeger's father went to Reno to obtain a divorce. Afterward, Seeger said, he

spent summers with his sons on the Patterson property. They lived in the barn, without a phone, electricity, or running water; they slept out and had picnics;
and each summer they had projects, building models
of boats or airplanes. When they drove to the beach,
Seeger and his brother John would sing harmonies in
the backseat of the car. In 1928, a young woman
named Ruth Crawford arrived as his father's secretary. "He was writing a book on dissonant counterpoint," Seeger said. "Most counterpoint is lovely
chords, major and minor, but a dissonant counterpoint is when you have a C sharp for one high note
and a C natural for the low note. The future of the
world will be full of dissonance as the world gets more
and more full of arguments, my father thought, and to
bring out the contrariness the counterpoint will have

to be more strident. They were trying partly to imitate Schoenberg and Charles Ives and a man in New York named Hanns Eisler who had written songs with Brecht. It was full of what a friend of mine called 'German stamping music,' and it turned out that the proletariat wasn't interested. My father was developing what he called musicology, I think he invented the term. Scientific writing about music is what it was, which was a term from Germany."

Meanwhile, the librarian in Nyack gave Seeger novels by Ernest Thompson Seton, who started the Boy Scouts. "Camping and woodcraft," Seeger said. "The first one I really liked was called *Rolf in the Woods*. Rolf was thirteen years old in 1810. He was being beaten by his stepfather, and his mother dies. He runs away and finds in the woods a wigwam with an old Indian living in it, trapping animals and exchanging their skins at the hardware store for tools and nails. The boy asks if he can stay with him, and the Indian points to a corner, and the boy falls asleep. The father comes along later and says, 'I see you're with the Indian, I'll go get my gun,' so the Indian and the boy run off together, and they end up in the Adirondacks. They make a little cabin and live there several years and take their skins into the nearest town. In 1812 along comes a war, and they're asked to be scouts on the Canadian border against the English. There is a description of a battle that is unforgettable. The English colonel thinks that the Americans will run out of ammunition, and he keeps sending his troops across the bridge until the water below is red with their blood. The Americans have much more ammunition than he thinks. The colonel realizes he's in trouble. It's a hair-raising closeup glance at what happens in war. I forgot to say that Rolf had earlier freed an English soldier who had caught his foot in a bear trap. He is then running across the bridge when he hears an English soldier say halt. It's the soldier Rolf had freed. He says, 'Run, Rolf, I'll shoot over your head.' Rolf's now fifteen. Anyway, you can see how it goes."

Seeger's brother Charles joined the Boy Scouts, "but I thought it was for the birds," Seeger said, "lining up in rows and saluting the flag." Seeger bought thirty-two yards of muslin fabric and had a seamstress sew him a rectangle twelve feet by twenty-four feet that he could use to make a teepee. Among the photographs on Seeger's wall is one of him as a scrawny little boy, without a shirt, and holding a bow and arrow. "Me pretending to be an Indian," he said.

Seeger's father married Ruth Crawford, who became a modernist composer. They moved to Maryland, and began working in Washington. In 1932, Seeger was enrolled at Avon Old Farms, a boys' school in Connecticut. His family had scraped together the money to send him, hoping that he would earn a scholarship. The woman who had started the school admired Cotswold architecture, and the school had slate roofs and dark oak interiors and stone walls.

Seeger had parts in the school plays. He was small and thin, "so with my hair curled and falsies, I played the female parts—in *Hamlet,* and *St. Joan,* by George Bernard Shaw." Also, Consuelo, the bare-backed tango queen, in *He Who Gets Slapped,* by a playwright named Leonid Andreyev, Consuelo being, according to the author, "a dainty little thing of seventeen or eighteen touched but lightly by the veneer of her environment," which was a traveling circus in Europe. In addition, he played tenor banjo in the school's five-piece jazz band.

"At Avon we had to do eight hours a week of community service," Seeger said. "Some kids chose the kitchen, but I chose the woods crew. There was a nice

French Canadian in charge of teaching us how to sharpen the ax with a file, and how to chop without hurting ourselves. He'd go through a piece of forest and blaze a tree that had to come down, a weeding process, and we'd cut them. The school also had a farm, and one week a year we'd spend at the farm. Getting up at four, doing chores—that's where I learned to milk a cow."

Before long Seeger was given a scholarship. Mainly what earned it, he said, was his having started a newspaper, the *Avon Weekly Newsletter,* which he wrote and mimeographed and sold for five cents. "It was an unusual scholarship," he said. "The woman who paid the bills for the school said that all she got from the school reports was the news, but from me she got the gossip." He had read the autobiography of Lincoln Steffens, a muckraker, and decided that he wanted to be a journalist. One of the teachers knew the playwright and poet Edna St. Vincent Millay, and when the school performed one of her plays she came to see it. "They told me that with my newspaper I should interview her," Seeger said. "I had never interviewed anyone famous. I didn't have the faintest idea what to ask. I didn't know she'd supported Sacco and Vanzetti, and supported free love. Later she was deeply in love with a businessman in Belgium who left his business, and they lived in Columbia County, not far from here, until he died, and she didn't live too much longer. Anyway, finally I blurted out, 'What do you think of Shakespeare?' I don't remember anything else of the interview."

In Washington, Seeger's father had begun working with John Lomax, who was making collections of American songs. The inspiration had come from the example of Francis James Child, who had collected English and Scottish ballads in the nineteenth century. Seeger's father and Lomax had encouraged Seeger's interest in the banjo—"He just *looked* like a banjo," Lomax said later. With his father one summer, Seeger made a trip to North Carolina to hear vernacular music. Describing the trip in his book *The Incompleat Folksinger,* Seeger wrote, "We wound down through the narrow valleys with so many turns in the road that I got seasick. We passed wretched little cabins with half-naked children peering out the door; we passed exhibits of patchwork quilts and other handicrafts which often were the main source of income. I first became acquainted with a side of America that I had never known before.

"At the Asheville square dance and ballad festival I fell in love with the old-fashioned five-string banjo, rippling out a rhythm to one fascinating song after another. I liked the rhythms. I liked the melodies, time-tested by generations of singers. I liked the words.

"Compared to the trivialities of the popular songs my brothers and I formerly harmonized, the words of these songs had all the meat of human life in them. They sang of heroes, outlaws, murderers, fools. They weren't afraid of being tragic instead of just sentimental. They weren't afraid of being scandalous instead of giggly or cute. Above all, they seemed frank, straightforward, honest. By comparison, it seemed to me that too many art songs were concerned with being elegant and too many pop songs were concerned with being clever."

AFTER THREE YEARS at Avon Old Farms, Seeger went to Harvard on a scholarship. "I roomed right above the Harvard Union, which was a big dining hall, and I made a little bit of money as a waiter," he said. "Then I went to a place where I could get free meals if I washed pots."

By the end of his sophomore year, he was on academic probation. If he failed, he would lose his scholarship. Instead, he left. "I wasn't sorry to leave Harvard," he said. "I was disgusted by what I considered the cynicism displayed by one of my professors. He would say, 'Every society has a spring, a winter, a summer, and a fall,' and scoff at us trying to stop Hitler. He said, 'All you can do is accommodate.' I was young and idealistic." Crossing the campus shortly before he departed, he passed one of his classmates, John F. Kennedy. "He was walking with someone who was carrying papers for him, I think, and saying something about being very annoyed at not having been able to reach someone on the phone."

The conversation returned to his father. Under a pseudonym, he said, his father wrote music columns for the *Daily Worker*. He gathered a group of musicians and composers, including Aaron Copland, and called it the Composers' Collective: "He figured there was a workers' collective. Why not one for musicians?" The Composers' Collective concerned itself with writing music for strikes and unemployment lines, and with music for the new world order. The music that already existed, especially folk music, they regarded as a relic, because it had existed before Karl Marx. They held a contest for the best May Day song, which Copland won with a song called "Into the Street May 1," which required a piano. Charles Seeger acknowledged that Copland's song was better than his own, but his was more practical, he said. The songs were marching songs, and how were marchers supposed to manage a piano?

Despite being skeptical of folk music, Charles liked Appalachian music—Seeger said that he might have helped inspire Copland to write "Appalachian Spring." "He brought up from Kentucky a woman named Aunt Molly Jackson," Seeger said. "Her father had been a member in the Knights of Labor, and when the Communists came along and led a strike in the mines in Harlan County, in 1932, she and her half brother and sisters not only were working hard trying to get the strikers to win, but they were making up songs. She sang, 'I am a union woman, just brave as I can be. I don't like the bosses, and they don't like me.' Her sister Kim wrote, 'I don't want your millions, mister, I don't want your diamond ring,' and her younger sister wrote, 'I hate your capitalist system, and I'll tell you the reason why,' and they were blacklisted when the strike was lost, and they moved to New York. Molly gave speeches and got a small apartment on the Lower East Side. My father brought her to the Composers' Collective, and said, 'Her songs are being taken up, and ours are not, we should listen to her,' but the collective said, 'She's music of the past.' My father said, 'I know some young people who will like to hear it,' and that's how I began to hear folk music written by the same people who were singing it."

As for the Composers' Collective, the closest they got to writing songs was when they wrote rounds, Seeger said. "My father wanted to publish a book called *Rounds About the Very Rich*. He was fond of one that was sung in three parts, like 'Row, Row Your Boat.' It went like this." Seeger put down his fork and, with his chin raised, began to sing, "Oh Joy upon this earth to live and see the day, when Rockefeller senior shall up to me and say, 'Comrade, can you spare a dime? Oh . . . ' "

Seeger's father believed that music's most important purpose was social. For a while in Washington he worked for the WPA music project. He wrote out a list of observations to which he gave the title "The Purposes of Music." Seeger went upstairs to a loft where he keeps his office to look for a copy. I heard him going through papers. "What did I do with that file," he said? "What did I do? This is ridiculous. Absolutely ridiculous . . . Aah—here it is." He came downstairs and handed it to me. The first principle was, "Music, as any art, is not an end in itself, but is a means for achieving larger ends." Another was, "Music as a group activity is more important than music as an individual accomplishment." Another was, "To *make* music is the essential thing—to listen to it is accessory." The musical culture of a nation should be judged not by the abilities of its best musicians, he wrote, but by how many people take part in making music. He also said that the important question to ask was not "Is it good music?" but "What is music good for?"; "and if it bids fair to aid in the welding of the people into more independent, capable and democratic action, it must be approved."

Seeger's father quit the Communist Party in 1938, when he read the transcripts of the Moscow Trials and concluded that the testimony had been forced. He devoted himself then to musicology. "He wrote papers he'd read at scholarly meetings," Seeger said. "If people didn't ask him questions, he'd question them—What did you think of the second paragraph? and so on. He had a kind of microphone that he used as a hearing aid, and he'd hold it up to them. Then he'd ask someone else, 'What did you think of what he said?' " Seeger sat back in his chair and shook his head. "That was fifty years ago," he said. "My god."

Then he stood up abruptly and said, "I forgot the pear tart." He brought the tart to the table, then he went to the freezer and came back with a column of ice cream containers—the Seegers had recently had a birthday party. While we ate the tart and the ice cream we got to talking about all the beautiful stone walls there are in the countryside around Beacon.

"In my mind's eye there's two teenagers, and the father's saying, 'Boys, you get ten feet of wall built, or you don't get any supper,' " Seeger said. "And one of them says to the other, 'Next year I'll be fourteen, and I'm going to get a job at the factory—they pay you two dollars a week. He don't see that much money in a month.' The father says, 'What will I do without you? The farm will go back to forest.' "

Seeger finished his tart and put his hands in his lap, like a penitent. "The opening of the American West meant the reforestation of the East," he said. "That's important." Then he began collecting the dishes.

IN THE SUMMER of 1938, having left Harvard, Seeger rode his bicycle west and made the watercolors of the farmhouses from the fields. (Years later, after he was famous, he would sometimes receive letters asking if he was the Seeger who had painted the barn the wrong color.) The following winter, when he was twenty, he moved to New York City. He still hoped he might become an artist or a journalist, but he was also beginning to think of becoming a musician. He was one of a collection of young artists who met periodically in a loft near Fourteenth Street and built puppets. In the summer, as the Vagabond Puppeteers, they drove through upstate New York in a car with a folding stage built onto one side of it, playing at hotels, and at a county fair, a street dance, a church picnic, for 4-H clubs, at schools, and for the gathering of a religious organization called Christian Endeavor. They charged ten dollars for a booking, but half the time they passed the hat instead. Their highest take, at a school fair, was $11.80; their lowest was $.83, for three appearances at a country fair where they performed in a sideshow along with a magician, a hermaphrodite, and a fire-eater. The bulk of their appearances were at picket lines and at meetings of dairy farmers who were on strike against the milk wholesalers. The farmers sometimes sat in the fields and shot holes in the scab milk trucks. "Farmers, when they get mad, get twice as mad as anybody," Seeger told me on another visit. For the strike meetings, the puppeteers had skits into which they would insert the names of local farmers. Seeger was the voice of a cow that would upbraid her owner for spending by necessity more money to feed and keep her than he did on his family. Between acts he would step out front and sing "The Farmer Is the Man," and a cotton farmers' song from 1920 called "Seven-Cent Cotton and Forty-Cent Meat, How in the World Can a Poor Man Eat?" Seeger adapted it to "One-Dollar Milk and Forty-Cent Meat." He also adapted a Kentucky murder ballad called "Pretty Polly" to one called "Mister Farmer," in which he described how the farmers were cheated by the prosperous wholesalers.

According to a piece in the *Daily Worker,* the puppeteers traveled five thousand miles over two and a half months, slept outdoors and never ate in a restaurant, and came back to New York with $13.34. Of one appearance the reporter wrote, "Pete Seeger, the young 'traveling troubadour,' led the Assembly in a number of militant working class songs."

In 1939, Seeger met Toshi, when he showed up to help a folk dance troupe clean the skylights at its studio, and she was the only other person to appear. (They didn't go out with each other until 1942, though.) Nineteen thirty-nine is also the year that Seeger met Woody Guthrie, through a friend. Seeger and Guthrie each played one night in Manhattan at a midnight benefit. "I sang one song very amateurishly and got polite applause and retired in dismay and confusion," Seeger told me. "Then Woody came on, and he was the star. He told jokes and sang a song, and he had his cowboy hat tilted back on his head." Alan Lomax–John Lomax's son, who worked with his

father—was in the audience, and he insisted that Guthrie come to Washington and record every song he knew for the Library of Congress. Seeger went with him. "Woody let me tag along because I could accompany him on anything he played. I could see a chord change coming and add the right notes—not too many, just enough," he said. "Except for that, he thought I was very strange. I didn't drink or chase women. I struck him as very young for my age."

Toward the end of 1939, Seeger was persuaded by John Lomax to stop looking for work as a journalist and to come to Washington to transcribe recordings of American songs from the Library of Congress collection. Seeger thinks his father might have said to Lomax, "Could Peter be of any use to you in the library?" Lomax paid Seeger fifteen dollars a week from his own salary, and Seeger had a room for three dollars a week. When he wanted a proper meal he would ride his bicycle to his father's house. From the material he was given he was instructed to make two piles, one of music that had no special merit, and one of music that he thought would interest Lomax. Each week he listened to hundreds of records—English and Scotch-Irish ballads kept alive in the South, rural blues, farmer songs, widow's laments, millworker songs, soldier songs, sea chanties, slave songs, tramp songs, and coal miner songs. Toward the end of May, Guthrie arrived. Alan Lomax kept a file of protest songs that he wanted to make into a book, but his father thought the project was too controversial. Lomax gave the file to Seeger and Guthrie and suggested they do it. Mostly back in New York, over the course of a month or so, Seeger transcribed the songs and Guthrie wrote introductions for each, "sometimes a paragraph, sometimes two pages, off the top of his head," Seeger said, "no rewriting." Guthrie showed it to the writer Theodore Dreiser, who told him, "You have a lot of work to do before you can publish this." It was published finally in 1964, from a copy a friend had kept–Seeger no longer had one.

Guthrie had arrived in Washington driving a new Plymouth. He had bought the car on credit, making the first (and only) payment with money he'd earned from singing on the radio in New York. "He was paid two hundred dollars a week for about fifteen minutes of singing, which was a lot of money when a poor person's job paid ten or fifteen," Seeger said. He quit after three weeks, though, because the radio station didn't want him to sing the songs he wanted to sing, and he didn't want to sing the songs they wanted. "His wife, Mary, had brought the kids up from Texas, and they'd rented a little apartment, and she went back," Seeger said. "She told him, 'Woody, couldn't you have kept at it a little longer, and then we could have paid off some bills,' but he was obdurate."

IN JUNE, GUTHRIE AND SEEGER drove the Plymouth to Texas to visit Guthrie's wife and children, who were living in the Panhandle. There is an account of the trip in *Woody Guthrie: A Life,* by Joe Klein, which includes this handsome observation, "Both were private, dreamy men who seemed to reinforce each other's unworldliness." Klein says that one day Seeger and Guthrie stopped for lunch at a black café, where the owner wouldn't serve them. He assumed that if he did, other white men would arrive later and tear the place down. Another day, Seeger said, they picked up a hitchhiker who had one leg and called himself Brooklyn Speedy. To raise gas money, Speedy stood in front of a Woolworth's with a box of pencils. Before they left town, Speedy asked Seeger to buy him some paregoric, which had opium in it. Seeger, he said, should tell the druggist that he had a baby with a stomachache, and that when he was asked to sign his name, he shouldn't sign his real one. The druggist told Seeger that two ounces was enough paregoric to keep a baby asleep for two years. The bottle Seeger brought back, Speedy drank at once. "That was what he had for supper," Seeger said. Seeger asked what the paregoric did for him, and Speedy said, "It just makes me relax, and the world moves by me."

Guthrie's wife and children had a shotgun shack in Pampa, Texas. Seeger told Klein that it was "like a shantytown." It was "long and narrow like a trailer, maybe ten feet wide and thirty feet deep." One night, when some of Guthrie's relations came over, Guthrie's mother-in-law "grabbed Pete by the shoulder and shook him," Klein writes. " 'You've got to make that man treat my daughter right!' " she said.

"I didn't know what to do," Seeger told me. "I knew he wasn't being faithful, but Mary, incidentally, has never said a nasty word about Woody. She has only said, 'We were too young, I was only sixteen, and he wasn't much older.' Did they fight much? I don't remember them shouting at each other, but she got her points across. She later had a very happy marriage."

AS SEEGER MADE these remarks, we were standing in the yard between the cabin and the house. The yard is flat, and there are three tall trees, so that when you arrive, you have to steer your car around them. In the winter, when Seeger's children were young, he flooded the yard and made a skating rink, and they skated in and out of the trees. We had just got out of Seeger's truck, which runs on electric power. Seeger was planning to dig a hole for a fence post and had bought a sack of cement in Beacon to hold the post fast. He left the cement in a wheelbarrow near the front door, because he was afraid that if he put it in his barn he'd forget about it. Seeger's short-term memory is not what he wishes it were anymore, but he easily recalls the names of writers and books and things he has read and figures from the past. It was late winter and in the woods around the house were white plastic buckets collecting sap from taps sunk into the maple trees. "I used to put out seventy," he said. "Then fifty, then forty, now it's many fewer. I've left it too late, though. It was too cold to start before, now it's been too warm."

Seeger parted from Guthrie in Texas after a few

days, he said. In his memoir and songbook *Where Have All the Flowers Gone,* he wrote that Guthrie had taught him "a half dozen well-known commercial country songs worth a quarter in any Western bar." Guthrie had instructed Seeger to enter a bar carrying his banjo, buy a beer, and nurse it. Before long someone would point at the banjo and ask if he could play it. Seeger was to say, "Maybe, a little," and keep to his beer. Sooner or later someone would say, "Kid, I got a quarter for you if you'll pick us a tune," and that was when it was time to play.

Seeger hitchhiked north, to Butte, Montana, then to Chicago and then to Alabama, where he registered for the draft in Scottsboro. Working toward New York, he went through Harlan County, Kentucky, to see the coal towns, sometimes riding freight trains.

Farmers depended on the men who rode them to harvest their crops. "The crops couldn't be brought in without migratory labor, and the migratory labor came on freight trains," Seeger said. "You'd start in Kansas, then work north to Nebraska, and then to North and South Dakota as the season unfolded."

Seeger caught his first train in St. Joseph, Missouri, and with about twenty men in an open boxcar rode nearly to Lincoln, Nebraska. One of the others told him as a rule to leave a train before the railroad police, called yard bulls, came to check it. In Lincoln, someone said, there was a policeman who liked to shoot hoboes off the trains. Seeger had never jumped from a train before. He thinks that impatience accounted for his leaving the train before it had slowed sufficiently. Landing awkwardly, he broke the neck of his banjo. He had with him a camera that he exchanged in Rapid City, South Dakota, for a five-dollar guitar in a pawnshop, and in three days he had made enough money singing in saloons to get his camera back. ("I had mailed the banjo to someone to be fixed," he said, "and I never saw it again.")

In a bar in Montana, a slurry old man asked if he knew all the verses to "Strawberry Roan." Seeger said he didn't, and the man insisted on dictating them, twenty-three verses in all. "It took us nearly as many bottles of beer to complete the job," Seeger wrote. In Butte, a miners' union asked him to sing on a night when he was planning to catch a train. The tracks

were at the foot of a hill. Seeger heard the train whistle as he took the stage. He sang a few songs hastily and was given a check for five dollars, which a bar downstairs from the meeting room converted into silver dollars. As he ran down the hill the silver dollars kept falling out of his pocket and rolling away in the dark. Eventually, he lost one of them. "It was 20 percent of my total capital, but I really wanted to catch that train," he wrote. For the next few hours the train he boarded was switched from one siding to another. In the morning, he woke still in Butte.

RETURNING TO NEW YORK, Seeger heard of a man named Lee Hays who had compiled a book of union songs. Hays had been a student at a progressive school in Arkansas named Commonwealth College, "until it was burned down by the Klan, in 1940," Seeger said. He came north because friends had told him that New York was the place to get a book published. The door of Hays's apartment was answered by his roommate, Mill Lampell. Before long, Seeger, Lampell, Hays, and Guthrie were performing as the Almanac Singers. The membership was fluid. Not infrequently, whoever among their friends happened to be around when a job was imminent was an Almanac Singer. Sometimes only Seeger showed up for a performance, sometimes they performed without him, and sometimes as many as five or six musicians performed. Guthrie described them as pretty good "for a group that rehearses on-stage." For a time the Almanacs were only Seeger and Guthrie. In 1977, the two of them were recalled in a newspaper story by a writer named Esther McCoy who met them during the summer of 1941, in Mexico, when her husband encountered them at a party at Theodore Dreiser's house and invited them to visit him and his wife in a cottage they had rented for the summer by the beach. To her and her husband's surprise, they showed up the following morning in a car that McCoy described as a "five passenger ruin."

"Pete was a slat of a lad, all Adam's apple and large trusting eyes," McCoy wrote, "with sudden attacks of embarrassment that reddened his cheeks . . . Woody was as light and wiry as one of the early planes made of sticks and canvas, and he was as light on his feet as a cat avoiding trouble." A characteristic element of their friendship was their tendency to work each other's nerves. "I can't stand him when he's around, but I miss him when he's gone," Seeger said of Guthrie.

Guthrie tended to write down lyrics as they came to him on whatever paper was at hand. On a plane he would write about people in the towns below and what they would think when they saw the plane, Seeger said. Or about the stewardess and whether she was meeting the pilot after the plane landed. He'd then, typically, leave the writing behind on the seat. Seeger would collect it and give it to him. "Do you have any idea how much Lee and I envy you?" Seeger would ask.

An agent in New York arranged an audition for the Almanac Singers at the Rainbow Room, the nightclub on top of one of the towers at Rockefeller Center. "The nightclub manager wanted the men to wear overalls, and the women to wear bonnets," Seeger said. "Woody thought working commercially was not much, and he was getting drunk and putting the fancy silverware in his pockets. Then he began to improvise verses." Seeger began to sing, "At the Rainbow Room the soup's on to boil, they're stirring the salad with Standard Oil." And: "The Rainbow Room it's mighty high, you can see John D. a-flyin' by." "That kind of thing," he said. "Oh, and, 'It's sixty stories high, they say, a long way back to the U.S.A.' " They didn't get the job. "Right after that we were red-baited in one of the New York papers, and the agent quit trying to get us any work," Seeger said. He shook his head slightly. "Seventy years ago," he said. "Think of it."

SEEGER WAS DRAFTED in 1942, during a period in which he was plagued by what the painter Gerald Murphy called "feelings of lowered consequence." His belief that a future in music would follow from a superfluity of talent—what he described in a letter as "unschooled genius"—had been undone by an awareness that he would have to work very hard. Dunaway writes that the shadow cast by his mother's bias toward classical music left Seeger wondering whether he would ever produce anything that would be taken seriously. To Toshi, Seeger wrote, "There have been so many failures. You don't know. Every song I started to write and gave up was a failure. I started to paint because I failed to get a job as a journalist. I started singing and playing more because I was a failure as a painter. I went into the army as willingly as I did because I was having more and more failure musically."

He was sent to Keesler Field, in Mississippi, where he learned "the hydraulic system of the B-24 bomber," he said. The other soldiers called him New York. He was kept in Mississippi six months longer than he

might have been, because Military Intelligence was skeptical of his opinions. They opened his mail and then questioned him. On a furlough he and Toshi were married, and in 1944 he was sent to Saipan, an island thirteen miles long and six miles wide, with a small mountain in the center of it. On the troopship he sang for the soldiers. "I was amazed at how many songs people could stumble through," he said. "Barbershop songs. 'Volga Boatmen.'"

His and Toshi's child, a boy, Peter Ohta Seeger, was born in August 1944. Seeger never saw him. "He was eleven months old, or was it ten," he said. "I was ten thousand miles away, so I couldn't comfort her, but her parents were here. He was born without a gall bladder, so once he got off milk, he couldn't digest food. He'd have seizures. No one knew until after his death."

ONE DAY I ARRIVED toward the end of the morning, and Seeger and I talked in the yard for a while and then we went into the house. Toshi said, "Pete, you didn't have any breakfast," and he said, "I had a cookie." She had left some soup out for us. While we ate, Seeger said that after he came home from the Army, around 1948, he began singing with three friends—Lee Hays, Fred Hellerman, and a young woman named Ronnie Gilbert—and they called themselves the Weavers. They performed at parties for their friends and at gatherings for left-wing causes and were broke and about to go separate ways in 1949 when Seeger persuaded a man named Max Gordon, who had a club called the Village Vanguard, to hire them for what he had once paid Seeger. They began in December of 1949, singing Christmas songs. The engagement lasted six months. By February, hardly anyone was coming to the club. Alan Lomax brought Carl Sandburg to hear them, and the remarks he made about them attracted the attention of newspaper editors and, then, a dependable audience. They made their first recording, "Tzena, Tzena," an Israeli song, in

May of 1950, when Seeger was thirty-one. Shortly after that, their recording of Leadbelly's "Goodnight, Irene" sold a million copies. The interest that followed was such that Toshi told me, "We gave up eating out in the city. Pete's too modest to tell you." When the Weavers went on their first tour, Toshi went with them as manager, reluctantly. Seeger had thought he couldn't do without her. They left their children in Beacon, in the care of Toshi's mother and father and were gone for six months. When they returned, their son, Danny, who was four, said he didn't recognize them. Toshi never left the children again.

Within a year, the Weavers had sold four million records. Seeger didn't enjoy being famous, and he didn't like being in show business, either. He told the magazine *Time,* "It's not so much fun now." He said he had been happier in the clubs, where "we could improvise, sing what we felt like singing." People would ask if it wasn't terrific finally to be successful. "I thought to myself, we were just as successful in 1941 when we sang 'Union Maid' for ten thousand striking transport workers," Seeger told me. "But those months of early 1950 were an interesting experience. Millions of teenagers first heard the words 'folk song.' "

Late in the spring of 1950, the Weavers were offered a television show. They signed a contract, but before the network signed it, a right-wing organization called Counterattack published a pamphlet with the title "Red Channels: The Report of Communist

Influence in Radio and Television," which listed 151 men and women whom they insinuated, by their associations, were Communists. The people named included Leonard Bernstein, Arthur Miller, Aaron Copland, Gypsy Rose Lee, and Orson Welles. Seeger was cited thirteen times, mostly for having sung for organizations that the editors of Counterattack regarded as suspicious.

" 'Red Channels' came out, and the contract was torn up," Seeger said. "I expected it, so I didn't really feel resentful. We assumed that sooner or later they'd get us." The Weavers continued to perform until 1952. In 1955, they got back together. Seeger left in 1957, "because the Weavers wanted to do a commercial for a cigarette company. I didn't think that was a very good idea. We took a vote, and it was three to one, so I did the commercial then the next day I recommended one of my students, Erik Darling, and he took over. Anyway, it was like being a member of a family, and I couldn't be a member of two families."

SEEGER'S POLITICS are of the most extravagantly conservative kind. He believes ardently in the Constitution and the Bill of Rights. His interpretation of them is literal. In his years of activism, through the movements for workers' rights, civil rights, the movement against the Vietnam War, and the ecological movement, in all of which he figured prominently, there is no conceit that he has more emphatically embraced than that all human beings are created equal and have equal rights. In the early and middle parts of the twentieth century, such a conviction made a person not a patriot, but a socialist. When Seeger moved to Beacon, in 1949, he held a couple of meetings with a middle-age couple, the only other Communists around, then quit the party. "I thought it was pointless," he said. "I realized I could sing the same songs I sang whether I belonged to the Communist Party or not, and I never liked the idea anyway of belonging to a secret organization."

After lunch we went out and looked at the river, and I could see where Seeger had been standing, in 1955, when a car arrived, and the man driving it asked if he was Pete Seeger. Then he handed Seeger an envelope and left. Seeger opened the envelope and called out to Toshi, "They've finally got around to me." He had been summoned to testify before the House Un-American Activities Committee, in August.

Toshi found a lawyer who told Seeger that the option most commonly invoked was to cite the Fifth Amendment, which would lead to the case's being dismissed. Seeger didn't care for the inference of guilt that the gesture implied. People who had done so were sometimes described as "Fifth Amendment Communists." The lawyer also said that Seeger could choose to talk about himself to the committee but refuse to talk about other people. "I had known I could do that," Seeger told me, "because my father, in 1952, I think it was, had to resign his job in Washington when the FBI came and spoke to him, and he said, 'I'm willing to undress myself in a sentence, but I'm not going to tell about anyone else I know.' They said, 'You've got to tell about everyone.' He said he wasn't willing to do that. He knew he would be fired, so he walked in the next morning and resigned. He was head of the music department of the Pan American Union. He'd hoped to hang on for a few years, since he hadn't the savings, but he closed down his house—a great big house that he'd raised four kids in—and his wife had just died a few months earlier, and my sister was going to Radcliffe, so he went up and got a crowded little apartment in Cambridge. Anyway, the lawyer told me if, at the hearing, I answered the question, 'Are you a member of the Communist Party?' the next question would be, 'Who did you know?' "

The third choice was to rely on the First Amendment, which guarantees freedom of speech and "the right of the people peaceably to assemble, and to petition the Government for a redress of grievances." The Hollywood Ten, a group of screenwriters and producers, had tried this in 1947, and been convicted of contempt, jailed for a year, and then blacklisted. Employing this tactic, Seeger might spend years in court, have his career ruined, and still go to jail. The lawyer left the choice to Seeger. He told him not to bait the committee, to be polite, to answer their questions, or say why he wouldn't. Refusing to answer would result in a contempt citation, and each citation could be worth a year in jail. As the hearing approached, the lawyer reviewed with Seeger the questions he was likely to be asked.

Seeger appeared before the committee, in New York, on August 18, 1955. He was interrogated by Walter Tavenner, the committee counsel; Representative Francis Walter, the chairman; Gordon Scherer, a congressman from Ohio and a former prosecutor; and Edwin Willis, a congressman from Louisiana. "They were small-town politicians," Seeger said. "Walter was a lawyer from the coal country."

Seeger wore a tweed jacket, a plaid shirt, a yellow

tie, and dark pants. Toshi sat in the audience, with his banjo. The men asked what Seeger did for a living. Student of American folklore, he said, but he made his living as "a banjo picker." Before going into the Army, had he practiced his profession?

"It is hard to call it a profession," Seeger said. "I kind of drifted into it and I never intended to be a musician, and I am glad I am one now, and it is a very honorable profession, but when I started out actually I wanted to be a newspaperman, and when I left school—"

"Will you answer the question, please?" Tavenner asked.

"I have to explain that it really wasn't my profession," Seeger said. "I picked up a little change in it."

"Did you practice your profession?"

"I sang for people, yes, before World War II, and I also did as early as 1925."

"And upon your return from the service in December of 1945, you continued in your profession?"

"I continued singing, and I expect I always will," Seeger said.

Tavenner was maneuvering Seeger toward admitting that he had sung for the Communist Party. Then he would ask him to name all the other people who had done the same thing or to name people who had listened to him. He referred to an announcement in the *Daily Worker* from 1947 which read, "Tonight—Bronx, hear Peter Seeger and his guitar, at Allerton

Section housewarming." Was the Allerton Section a section of the Communist Party, Tavenner asked?

Seeger refused to answer. When pressed, he said, "I am not going to answer any questions as to my association, my philosophical or religious beliefs or my political beliefs, or how I voted in any election, or any of these private affairs. I think these are very improper questions for any American to be asked, especially under such compulsion as this. I would be very glad to tell you my life if you want to hear of it."

They didn't. Tavenner asked instead if Seeger had performed at a May Day Rally in 1948.

"I believe I have already answered this question, and the same answer," Seeger said.

Walter asked what that answer was.

"I feel that in my whole life I have never done anything of any conspiratorial nature," Seeger said, "and I resent very much and very deeply the implication of being called before this committee that in some way because my opinions may be different from yours, or yours, Mr. Willis, or yours, Mr. Scherer, that I am any less of an American than anybody else. I love my country very deeply, sir."

"Why don't you make a little contribution toward preserving its institutions?" Walter asked.

"I feel that my whole life is a contribution," Seeger said. "That is why I would like to tell you about it."

"I don't want to hear about it," Walter said.

Scherer asked that Seeger be directed to answer, a formality. Each time a witness was directed to answer and didn't, he was regarded as being in contempt. Seeger said he had already answered.

"Let me understand," Scherer said. "You are not relying on the Fifth Amendment, are you?"

"No, sir," Seeger said, "although I do not want to in any way discredit or depreciate or depredate the witnesses that have used the Fifth Amendment, and I simply feel it is improper for this committee to ask such questions."

"And then in answering the rest of the questions," Scherer said, "or in refusing to answer the rest of the questions, I understand that you are not relying on the Fifth Amendment as a basis for your refusal to answer?"

"No, I am not, sir."

Tavenner continued to ask about events where Seeger was said to have taken part. Seeger would say, "My answer is the same as before," and Scherer would say, "I think we have to have a direction." When a song was mentioned, Seeger would offer to sing it, and he would be rebuffed.

Some ways into their discourse, Tavenner gave Seeger a photograph, taken at a May Day parade in New York, in 1952, in which Seeger is wearing an Army uniform, and carrying a sign that says "Censored."

"Will you examine it, please, and state whether or not that is a photograph of you?" he asked.

Seeger looked at the photograph. "It is like Jesus Christ when asked by Pontius Pilate, 'Are you king of the Jews?' " Seeger said.

As if admonishing a child, Chairman Walter said, "Stop that."

"Let someone else identify that picture," Seeger said.

"I ask that he be directed to answer the question," Scherer said.

"I direct you to answer the question," Chairman Walter said.

"Do I identify this photograph?" Seeger asked.

Walter said, "Yes."

"I say let someone else identify it."

The Protest Singer

. . .

STANDING ON THE LAWN, I asked Seeger what he had meant by that answer. "I'd always been amused by the 'Thou sayest' retort," he said. " 'Are you king of the Jews?' 'So you sayest.' I think I probably had thought of it if somebody asked, 'Are you a Communist?' "

THE COMMITTEE GREW IMPATIENT with Seeger's intransigence. Tavenner tried once more to have him identify himself in the photograph. Walter directed him to answer. "The same answer, sir, as before," Seeger said.

When Scherer said, "We are not accepting the answers or the reasons you gave," Seeger said, "That is your prerogative, sir."

"Do you understand it is the feeling of the committee that you are in contempt as a result of the position you take?" Scherer asked.

"I can't say," Seeger said.

Seeger testified for nearly an hour more, with no deviation from form. At one moment the committee appeared to think it had cornered him, because he had said that he sang for "everybody." Well, if for everybody, then Communists among them?

"My answer is the same as before."

"What is that?" Walter asked.

After consulting with his lawyer, Seeger said, "I decline to discuss, under compulsion, where I have sung, and who has sung my songs, and who else has sung with me, and the people I have known. I love my country very dearly, and I greatly resent this implication that some of the places that I have sung and some of the people that I have known, and some of my opinions, whether they are religious or philosophical, or I might be a vegetarian, make me any less of an American. I will tell you about my songs, but I am not interested in telling you who wrote them, and I will tell you about my songs, and I am not interested in who listened to them."

Before much longer Tavenner said, "I have no further questions, Mr. Chairman," and Chairman Walter said, "The witness is excused."

SEEGER LEFT THE HEARING knowing that he would be indicted for contempt of Congress, and on March 26, 1957, he was, by a federal grand jury, on ten counts. According to Dunaway, he told his friends, "I still feel I committed no wrong, and that my children will not feel ashamed of me in future years."

THE INDICTMENT SPECIFIED that he couldn't leave the southern district of New York without permission.

Brooklyn lies outside the southern district, and so does New Jersey. His lawyer managed to have the terms changed to notification, meaning that every time Seeger went somewhere to work, he had to send a telegram saying where he was going and how he was getting there. At one nightclub the announcer introduced him by saying, "Here's Pete Seeger, out on bail." Fewer clubs were willing to hire him. He had to go farther from home to work. Sometimes he would do four performances in a day at four different places.

In hotel rooms he had to open the doors of the closets to be sure that he wasn't about to be set up. The phone rang at all hours of the night, and often when he answered he heard a click or someone breathing or profanity. A group called Texans for America persuaded textbook publishers to remove any mention of him. Dunaway writes that a woman in Ohio who had him sing at a barbecue in her backyard received a summons from HUAC. He was to play two nights in Nyack. The American Legion discovered in time to prevent the second night's performance that the theater had an expired license. To renew it, the owner of the theater had to pay a fee. The town offices were shut before he could, and the mayor and the clerk left town.

More and more, Seeger sang at schools. Once, between the indictment and his trial, he was in Louisiana to give a concert when he was invited to sing at a party, where he was introduced to Congressman Willis, from the HUAC Committee. "He was

completely taken by surprise," Seeger said, "as was I. For a while he glowered in the corner, then he beckoned to me with his finger. We went into the kitchen and he said, 'Well, Mr. Seeger, it's a small world, isn't it.' He had married the daughter of the local sugar mill owner, so his father-in-law had charge of all the jobs in town." Willis wanted to know how Seeger had come to be in his district, and Seeger said he had been invited. Willis said he wasn't welcome. Seeger had been engaged to sing next day at the school, but Willis said he'd raise a fuss if he did. Having already performed at the concert that had brought him to town, and not wanting to make life difficult for the people who had invited him, Seeger left for his next booking, in Houston.

SEEGER'S TRIAL WAS HELD in March of 1961. The jury took twenty minutes to decide he was guilty and sentenced him to a year in jail. In May of 1962 the Court of Appeals ruled that the indictment was faulty and dismissed the case. As we stood in the yard, he quoted a line from the decision, " 'We are not inclined to dismiss lightly claims of constitutional stature because they are asserted by one who may appear unworthy of sympathy.' 'Unworthy of sympathy,' " he said again and shook his head.

Before the HUAC engagement, people sometimes regarded Seeger's optimism as childish, and unrealistic, as a habit of mind inconsistent with the moral rigor of a serious person. Afterward, he became a figure of undeniable stature. He had stared down jailtime. He had stood amid peril for his beliefs. He had typified the principles of all the brave people he sang about.

HE ESCAPED ONLY the formal part of his sentence. He was a guest on *Open End,* a television interview program, when someone in the audience asked how he knew he was blacklisted. He said that it was difficult to know, one knew mostly by inference, when the host, David Susskind, interrupted and said, "Mr. Seeger, I can tell you, you're blacklisted."

After being sentenced, Seeger accepted every job he was offered, hoping to earn enough money for his family to live for the year he'd spend in jail. He assumed that many of the jobs would be withdrawn. When they weren't, he found himself traveling almost endlessly, leaving Toshi with three small children and all the cares of the household. After he was exonerated, she said, "Next time, no appeal. You go to jail." Mostly Seeger played at small colleges, which weren't as susceptible as larger schools to government pressure. Many years later, Seeger told an interviewer that the blacklist was almost a blessing. "I was glad to leave the commercial world," he said. "I went back to singing for kids in schools, where I'd started at." About his time as a famous entertainer he said, "Oh, sure, the work in nightclubs was interesting . . . but by and large the commercial music experience—well, it's hard to find the words."

DESPITE TOSHI'S ADMONITION, the years of the blacklist were furiously itinerant. They also drew a boundary in Seeger's life. Beforehand, his devotion to workers' rights, derived from his father's principles, was single-minded. Afterward, his sympathies broadened, and he became a figure of influence in movements that were nascent, all of them sprung from within the context of his concerns for peace, right behavior, and human dignity.

The blacklist was demised in 1962, when a lawsuit made anyone who enacted it liable for lost wages, but it lingered indirectly for several more years. During this period, nearly every folk musician of any consequence performed on television, except Seeger. They tended to divide into two camps: those who would appear, and those who wouldn't unless Seeger was included. By the organizers of a dinner at the White House with President Kennedy, which was to be broadcast, he was invited to sing, but the invitation was rescinded. Advertisers wouldn't have him, he was told.

Partly to escape such an impoverishing atmosphere Seeger and Toshi decided to take their children on a trip around the world to hear vernacular musics played in their native environments. In the trade papers, Seeger's manager advertised the trip as a world tour. They left in the summer of 1963. To carry as little as possible and avoid being charged for extra luggage, everyone brought only two outfits, one to wear and one for the wash. They also had a movie camera and a tape recorder. Shortly before they left, Seeger was offered a place on a network show, but the network insisted that he sign a loyalty oath. He wrote to them, "I just finished a seven-year court battle to prove the principle that such oaths are unconstitutional, and I was acquitted and vindicated."

Seeger's plan was to earn enough money as the family traveled to buy airplane tickets to the next destination. Not everywhere was he sufficiently well known to draw an audience, however. Moreover, in many places he had to perform with an interpreter, which was awkward.

The family went first to Australia and then to Indonesia. "Everyone thought war was going to break out between Australia and Indonesia, and when we got to the hotel it was deserted," Seeger told me. "Tinya didn't know how to swim, but by the end of the week, with the hotel pool to ourselves, she did." In Japan they stayed for a month, and Toshi's father joined them, seeing his family for the first time in fifty years. In Java they heard a "wonderful gamelan orchestra with a state row of dancers," and their son, Danny, caught a fever and was very sick. In India perhaps sixty thousand people heard Seeger at a concert in a park. Kenya "seemed rich compared to Calcutta," Seeger told me, "where they picked dead bodies off the sidewalks every morning." Through the windows of a hired car they saw Dar es Salaam and Mount Kilimanjaro. In Ghana they accompanied fishermen who sang while they cast nets from canoes and then hauled them in. In Nigeria they visited a village chief. "We drove through a gate and into the courtyard while the guard played a phrase on a talking drum. When we got to the other side of the courtyard the leader came out, and I said, 'How did you know we were here?' He said the drummer had announced us. He said a person could say anything he wanted in their language on the drums. He pointed at a man across the courtyard and said, 'Ask the drummer to send him a message.' I said, 'Have him bring me that umbrella lying next to him,' and the man played the drum, and the other man, who was asleep actually, woke up and looked around and brought me the umbrella." They went to Israel and Italy, and drove through Germany without stopping, to Austria, where they attended the Winter Olympics, but almost all they saw was the backs of the people in front of them. In the end they were gone nearly a year and passed through thirty countries.

ABROAD, SEEGER HAD FELT that the most worth-
while thing he could do was to describe the civil
rights movement in America. (Had he made the trip
earlier, he might have described the work of the
unions, but "the union movement had been well
split," he told me, "the lefties had all been kicked out,
the movement was struggling along and not doing
well, and overseas I felt instead that everybody
should know about Dr. King.") Seeger had met King,
briefly, in 1957, "just to say hello," when each was
invited to the twenty-fifth anniversary of the Highlander Folk School, which had been started in Tennessee by a man named Myles Horton. The school
was a center for leftist thought. Seeger says that Horton had in mind "the example of Danish folk schools.
The idea being that any group of people who can
read can teach themselves. The ideal is seven or
eight, not too big or small. Every week you meet and
take turns reading a chapter and giving a report, and
the others ask questions. At the end of a year everybody's learned to make reports and ask questions."
Before the Montgomery bus boycott, Rosa Parks had
attended the Highlander School.

On his world tour, Seeger would talk about King,
and then he would sing "We Shall Overcome." The
record that included his version, made at Carnegie

Hall in 1963, sold half a million copies. Seeger had learned the song in 1947 from Zilphia Horton, a musician and activist and Myles Horton's wife. It had originally been a union song.

"In the *United Mine Workers Journal* of the year 1909 there was a long letter on the front page, February," Seeger told me, "and the letter said, At our strike meetings last year we started out each meeting with a prayer and that good old song, 'We Will Overcome.' They probably sang it fast. The song they took it from is 'I'll Be All Right.' 'I'll be like Him' is the second verse, 'I'll wear a crown' is third, and the last verse is 'I'll overcome.' It's still sung. However, in 1946, a woman named Lucille Simmons resurrected it for a tobacco workers' strike. She liked to sing it long-meter style, as well as fast and syncopated: any gospel song can be sung super slow, long-meter style. Lucille would come out of the picket line—maybe people were warming their hands around a fire in an oil drum—and they'd say, 'Here comes Lucille, she's going to sing that slow song,' and she sang it slower than anyone ever heard it.

"Long-meter style is the way Zilphia Horton learned it—why didn't her parents just call her Sylvia, I wonder—and she taught it to me, but I didn't know how to play it right. I just gave it a banjo accompaniment, and I didn't even sing it very much. Eventually I changed the Will to Shall. Toshi jokes that it's my college education, but I've always used shall in the first person. Are you going to town tomorrow? Yes, I shall. Anyway, shall opens up the mouth better; the short 'I' is not as dramatic a sound as the 'aah.' I taught the song to Frank Hamilton, who taught it to a young boy named Guy Carawan, and they put it in this twelve-eight meter, but slow, and that gave it that great, pulsating rhythm. I am not sure where Dr. King heard it, but there was a woman, what was her name, she died only last year, and she remembered driving Dr. King to a speech in Kentucky and him in the back-seat saying, ' "We Shall Overcome," that song really sticks with you, doesn't it.' "

After Seeger returned to America he sang when-ever he was asked at demonstrations and in southern churches and at voter registration drives in favor of civil rights. In footage from the period he is frequently one of the few and sometimes the only white person among a crowd. In early 1964, along with other enter-tainers, he went to Mississippi to visit some voter-registration projects. It was during the season when three student volunteers, two white and one black—Andrew Goodman, Michael Schwerner, and James Chaney—had gone missing, but before they had been found, two months later, buried in a backwoods dam. Flying to Jackson, Seeger sat with a reporter. When Seeger got off the plane, a man was "waiting for us, me and the reporter, in a little anteroom before we went into the airport, and he said, 'You come down here to sing for the niggers.' I said, 'I hope to sing for

everybody.' He wasn't interested. He'd been in the seat in front of me on the plane while I had been talking a little too frankly and carelessly. I think I made some flippant statement like, 'You know the KKK types want to see people killed, so it scares the others from acting out bravely.' And I remember him clenching. In the anteroom he said, 'You watch what you're doing. If we weren't here, I'd knock the shit out of you.' With the reporters around us, he didn't know what to do. I guess I was lucky."

In 1965, Seeger and Toshi, responding to an invitation from King, which had been distributed by telegrams to celebrated people, joined the third march from Selma to Montgomery. (The first, which was held to protest the shooting of a black man by a state trooper during a demonstration, and which included somewhere between five and six hundred people, had been turned back by the police after six blocks; because of the beatings the police inflicted the occasion was referred to as Bloody Sunday; the second, three weeks later, was intended as symbolic–a gesture until a court order was resolved. Even so, a minister from Boston was beaten outside a segregationist's café. The hospital close by said it was full, so he was driven to one a few hours away, where he died two days later.) The Seegers arrived on the march's fourth day. The line of people, five or six abreast, was a mile long. "We were keeping to one side of the highway, so traffic could get by," Seeger said, "and there were federal helicopters going overhead spying out snipers in the cornfield, and it was raining half the time. We had improvised raincoats out of plastic bags. A few people had umbrellas. And there were no public address systems, so there'd be fifteen people here singing one song, and a hundred feet later, people singing another song. I let Toshi walk steadily with one group, but occasionally I'd run up ahead of her and listen to songs in different places, so I heard a fairly wide variety of songs. I remember asking a woman if she knew the lyrics to one song and her laughing at me, saying, 'Don't you know you can't write down freedom songs, they change every time you hear them.' " Seeger and Toshi stayed the night in the marchers' camp while Seeger went around with a notebook, collecting lyrics.

Although Seeger was regarded as someone whose support arrived early in the movement's history and was steadfast, he quietly withdrew when he began to feel less certain of his place. For a time the movement appeared to him to be managed by white people, and that didn't seem proper. "I remember during what they called the Freedom Summer, 1964, being in a room in the South with about twenty-five white people and two black people and thinking, If I feel the balance is uneven then the people most directly concerned must feel that way, too," Seeger said. In addition, the movement had become more militant. "I was more at home with the followers of Dr. King than I was with the followers of Malcolm X," he said. "Reading about Martin Luther King really turned my philosophy around. He used to say, 'If you face an opponent on a broad front, you don't aim for the strong points, you aim for a weak one, but you take it.' On the other hand, Malcolm and Dr. King started working together more closely around the time Malcolm was murdered. Once King was gone, though, no one was able to pull the movement together, the way King had, because there were people who said, 'Look, if they're going to throw stones at us, we'll throw stones at them.' Stokely Carmichael and many others felt—well, they quoted Paul Robeson—somebody once

asked him, If somebody slapped you on one cheek,
would you turn the other cheek? 'No,' he said. 'If they
slapped me on one cheek, they wouldn't get around to
slapping me on the other.' King, however, had learned
from Gandhi, who had learned from Thoreau, and
they both quoted Jesus at times, 'Let he who is without sin cast the first stone.' Anyway, I began to think,
If they want me to come down, I'll come down, but I
tried not to push myself on anyone."

BEING BANISHED FROM network television, Seeger
filmed his own television show, in 1967, *Rainbow Quest,*
which was broadcast on several public television stations—New York, Miami, and San Francisco among

them. Toshi was the producer. Seeger would play and have as guests musicians such as Doc Watson, Johnny Cash and June Carter, Mississippi John Hurt, the Stanley Brothers, Reverend Gary Davis, Judy Collins, and Richard and Mimi Farina. Occasionally they showed home movies from Africa. The show was filmed in black-and-white in a studio in Newark. "There was a rather avant-garde type of scenery," Seeger said. "A door and a window with no wall next to them." The musicians sat around a table and played and talked. Johnny Cash took off his shoes, which seemed to be bothering him, and sang and played guitar in his socks. While Seeger talked to June Carter, Cash toyed with a cigarette lighter, then he dropped it and quickly picked it up and apologized sheepishly. Offstage, Toshi glared at him. Cash had arrived stoned on something, and she hadn't wanted to have him on at all. For most of the program he writhed in his chair, but his performance was superb.

Some of the shows preserved performances of musicians who might not have been filmed anywhere else. One episode featured an older musician named Roscoe Holcomb, from Kentucky, who played banjo and guitar and sang. Holcomb's past had included a lot of church singing. Although he was admired as a musician, he had mostly worked at other jobs.

"You make your living as a construction worker mainly?" Seeger asked.

"Yeah, a construction worker," Holcomb said.

There was a long pause.

"Well, I think it's wonderful," Seeger said. "I'm glad that you've taken time off from your other work to make this music here."

"Well, I've got now to where I can't work," Holcomb said. "I've had my back broke. The older I get, the worser I get, and I get to where I can't to now work hardly."

Then Holcomb, a somber figure in a suit and hat, like an undertaker, played a song. He had a high, nasal voice. While he played, images appeared on the screen of him working in his garden. Holcomb grew so diverted that he came to a dead stop. "Now you just take your eyes off the monitor and keep playing," Seeger said gently, and Holcomb started again. Seeger and Toshi continued with the program for as long as they could afford it. In all there were thirty-nine episodes. "If twenty stations had carried it, we would have broken even," he said. "I think twelve or thirteen carried it. The people who came to be on it never asked for a lot of money. Johnny Cash wouldn't take a penny."

Around this time, Seeger saw a newspaper photograph of soldiers fording a river, and the phrase "waist deep in the big muddy" came to him. It lent itself to the refrain of a song—"We're waist deep in the big muddy, and the big fool says to push on." The narrator is a soldier in Louisiana in 1942, whose captain insists on crossing a river the soldiers are reluctant to

cross and who drowns while doing so, but most people concluded that the subject was actually Vietnam,
and that the big fool was Lyndon Johnson. "It was an
allegory," Seeger told me, "and a very obvious one."
On tour in Europe, Seeger visited Russia, where in
Moscow a student asked if he would perform at his
university, because Seeger's concert in the city was
sold out. The *New York Times* correspondent, a man
named Peter Grose, asked Seeger if he could come to
the university concert with Seeger; otherwise, he
wouldn't be allowed on campus. Seeger let him carry
his guitar. The students asked what kind of music was
being played in the United States, and Seeger mentioned Dylan and Phil Ochs, and he sang "Waist
Deep in the Big Muddy." The *Times* published a piece
with the headline, "Seeger Sings Anti-American Song
in Moscow." Seeger called the editor of the *Times* and
read him the lyrics, and the editor agreed they were
not anti-American, but the harm was already done.
The Beacon paper printed the *Times* piece just as
Seeger was to sing at the Beacon High School, with
the result that seven hundred people signed a petition
against his appearing. In the woods at one end of his
property, someone set a fire. Seeger saw smoke and
called the fire department. The next week a fire was
set at the other end of the property. Even so, Seeger
decided to press the matter of his appearance. He was
cheered when one day on the street, the elderly owner
of a store, a Republican, stopped him and said, "I

don't know what your politics are, but you have a right to your opinion." The high school students wanted Seeger to perform, and the head of the school board said he could not legally prevent the school's being used. The New York Supreme Court had a few years earlier delivered a ruling that if schools rent their premises to anyone they must rent to everyone. Pointedly, the ruling was the result of a case brought on Long Island when the John Birch Society had tried to stop Seeger from appearing. The concert was well attended, Seeger thinks partly because of the publicity. The lesson he took from the encounter, he said, was that he needed to be as engaged in Beacon as he was elsewhere in the world.

In September of 1967, Seeger was finally invited to

sing on a network television show, the *Smothers Brothers Comedy Hour,* which was broadcast on CBS. The *Los Angeles Times* likened the invitation to "the glimmer of light at the end of what must seem to Seeger like an endless black tunnel." He had last appeared on network television in 1950, with the Weavers.

Seeger's performance was taped in Los Angeles. After he sang "Wimoweh," Tommy Smothers asked, "You going to do that song now?" They talked momentarily about the individual meanings of songs, then Smothers left the stage, and Seeger sang "Waist Deep in the Big Muddy." In the following days the tape was reviewed by the network's practices department in New York. The version that was broadcast showed Seeger playing the guitar, then the camera cut briefly to the audience, and when it returned to Seeger, he was playing the banjo. The network had simply scissored out the intervening minutes.

Seeger told a reporter from the *New York Times,* "I'm very grateful to CBS for letting me return to commercial broadcasting, but I think what they did was wrong, and I'm really concerned about it. I think the public should know that their airwaves are censored for ideas as well as for sex." The network dissembled, then abruptly invited Seeger to appear in February of 1968. He performed a medley of war songs—from the Revolution, from the Mexican War of 1848, from the Civil War, the Spanish-American War, and from World War I—then he sang "Waist

Deep in the Big Muddy" to approximately seven million people, his largest audience ever, although the
CBS station in Detroit deleted a verse.

Seeger's record company released "Waist Deep in
the Big Muddy" as a single, but it didn't sell as well as
he had hoped. He didn't care about the money; he
had thought the song could save the lives of soldiers.
Sometime after it came out he met a young man who
told him that he had worked in the office in Denver of
the regional distributor of his record company and
that when the record had arrived his boss had said
angrily that the executives in New York must be crazy
if they thought he could sell such a thing. The young
man told Seeger that "Waist Deep in the Big Muddy"
never left the shelves. Several weeks after Seeger's
appearance, Lyndon Johnson announced that certain
troops would return from Vietnam, and that he
wouldn't run for president again. Even if only
obliquely, Seeger feels that he played some role in the
decision.

A few years later, after Seeger had sung at a festival
near Beacon, a man approached as he was sitting with
Toshi and extended his hand. "Mr. Seeger, I think I
should tell you, I came here this afternoon to kill you,"
he said. Seeger was so startled that he thinks he managed to say only, "Thank you." Toshi said, "You must
speak to him." The man had been a soldier in Vietnam, and he regarded Seeger's embrace of peace as
the gesture of a traitor. As he sat through the concert,

laying eyes on Seeger for the first time, and singing with the rest of the audience, his antagonism dissolved. Seeger talked to him—he doesn't remember about what anymore—and they sang a song, and when they finished the man said, "I feel cleansed"— not rapturously, but of his hatred, Seeger told me. He discusses the encounter only reluctantly.

"MANY OF MY PROJECTS in life have failed, and Toshi has lived through so many of these failures with me," Seeger told me one day. "The *Clearwater* was the exception that proved the rule."

From reading *Silent Spring,* by Rachel Carson, in 1962, Seeger became aware of the fragility of the environment. Around the same time he began sailing a small boat on the Hudson River and was distressed by how filthy the water was. In 1963, from a friend, Vic Schwartz, Seeger heard about the sloops that sailed on the river in the eighteenth and nineteenth centuries. Their booms, Schwartz said, were seventy feet long. ("I thought only yachts in the America's Cup had booms that big," Seeger told me.) Schwartz lent him a book called *Sloops of the Hudson,* written in 1908, which Seeger read twice. A few years later he stayed awake one night typing a long letter to Schwartz proposing that they build a replica of a Hudson River sloop. He thought the boat would cost about a hundred thousand dollars, which people

would donate. Seeger mailed the letter then forgot about it. Four months later he met Schwartz on the Beacon train platform, and Schwartz asked, "When are we going to get started on the boat?" Seeger said, "What boat?" Schwartz reminded him of the letter. Seeger said, "Oh, that. That makes about as much sense as saying, 'Let's build a canoe and paddle to Tahiti.'" Schwartz said he had passed the letter around and about a dozen people had regarded the idea as a good one.

"They built a replica of the *Mayflower*," Seeger told me. "Why not build a Hudson River sloop?" He and Schwartz organized a committee. "Some people wanted the boat to be a purely historical project and dress the sailors in costumes, and others wanted it to be the centerpiece of a fighting environmental organization. I saw it as a middle-class project. Pretty soon there were arguments. Some people said, 'There's a war on, what are you doing building a boat?' and I didn't know what to say except, 'The river's worth saving.'"

The river carried clots of sewage and chemicals from factories and ships and boats and runoffs and outfalls. Restoring it to a river that someone could swim in safely seemed impossible. Seeger saw the sloop as a stage from which people could be taught about caring for the river. He assumed he could find a dilapidated boat and restore it. "I hunted around Long Island Sound for an original Hudson River sloop," he told an interviewer, "and the old-timers would say, 'Oh, there's one thirty feet away from you,' and I'd look around, and they'd add, ' . . . straight down. Sunk about fifty years ago.' " He decided he'd have to build a sloop, but the price from yachtmakers around New York was steeper than he and the committee could afford. In South Bristol, Maine, he found a shipbuilder named Harvey Gamage who said that he had built a lot of boats like the one Seeger proposed—but why did Seeger want an old-fashioned boat? Seeger said that he hoped to clean up the Hudson River, and Gamage, sympathetic, offered a price that was half what the New York shipbuilders had given. The *Clearwater* was drawn up by a naval architect named Cyrus Hamlin. It was to weigh a hundred tons, mostly of oak, be twenty-five feet wide, seventy-six feet long, have a mast a hundred and six feet tall, and carry the largest mainsail in the world. The keel was laid in 1968, and the *Clearwater* was launched in June of 1969.

"We sailed it for two or three days to make sure

everything was right, then we started down the coast," Seeger said. "Toshi had hired someone to set up concerts in a series of towns to raise money, so each day we would sail twenty or thirty miles and give a concert." After thirty-seven days, they reached New York.

Almost immediately Seeger began to remove himself from the center of the sloop's affairs. "I thought it very important that the *Clearwater* be everybody's boat," he said, "and there was too much publicity about me. Also, I was singing songs against the Vietnam War, and the vice president of the committee said, 'As long as Seeger is involved with this organization, we'll never get anywhere, because Seeger can't get along with the Establishment.' He's a friend of mine now, but we were just launched, and although the boat was paid for, we needed money for the insurance and the captain's salary, so I stepped aside."

When Seeger's daughter Tinya was a child, he told her that one day the river would be clean enough for her to swim in, and now it mostly is, for roughly a hundred and fifty miles between Coxsackie and Yonkers. (After a heavy rain, it isn't.) Seeger believed that if he could bring people to the river, they would see how beautiful it was. They would ask, Is it safe to swim in, with the result that they would want to be part of the effort to make it so. To attract them, he began holding festivals on the riverbank. There was one in Riverside Park, in New York City, while the *Clearwater* sailed back and forth on the river. In all the efforts Seeger has made, the renewed life of the river may be the one in which his unconquerable optimism, his resourcefulness, courage, and indefatigability counted the most. His ardent feelings for the river are not unexampled, nor is his commitment. Many people saved the river, but the way in which it was saved bears in large degree his philosophical signature. It exemplified his belief that people can be galvanized by appealing to their common interests.

"People ask, is there one word that you have more faith in than any other word," he told me, "and I'd say it's participation. I feel that this takes on so many meanings. The composer John Philip Sousa said, 'What will happen to the American voice now that the phonograph has been invented? Women used to sing lullabies to their children.' It's been my life work, to get participation, whether it's a union song, or a peace song, civil rights, or a women's movement, or gay liberation. When you sing, you feel a kind of strength; you think, I'm not alone, there's a whole batch of us who feel this way. I'm just one person, but it's almost my religion now to persuade people that even if it's only you and three others, do something. You and one other, do something. If it's only you, and you do a good job as a songwriter, people will sing it."

IN 1994, SEEGER WAS GIVEN an evening of honors at the Kennedy Center, in Washington, D.C., a kind of knighthood in the performing arts. In 1996 he was elected to the Rock and Roll Hall of Fame. In the fall of 2008 he released a new record, *At 89,* and he appeared on David Letterman. The second time I heard Seeger perform was during the spring of 2006, in Beacon at an elementary school, where he sang for an assembly. The room he sang in—it might also have been the cafeteria—had orange linoleum on the floor and a small stage at one end. I sat against a wall, on a folding chair, beside Toshi. The children arrived like an avid little flock. From the stage a man I took to be the principal said over a microphone, "Ms. Salvia's class, once you're seated, back up," and the children, almost impossibly delicate, walked forward two at a time then paired off like bridesmaids and lowered themselves to the floor. As if from the pressure of the principal's palms moving toward them, they slid backward. Another row of children stepped forward and replaced them. "Ms. Havershaw's class, once you're seated back up a little bit," and so on, the man said, until there were about twenty-five rows, with the smallest children in front. Meanwhile, Seeger sat on the floor beside us. Next to him was a little boy. Seeger extended his hand and said, "What's your name? I'm Pete." The boy gave his name, which I didn't hear, and solemnly shook Seeger's hand, as if they were making a pact.

The lights were lowered and the principal showed slides of Seeger standing in front of microphones at various demonstrations and with Woody Guthrie, his son, Arlo, and Bob Dylan. When he described Seeger as "probably the person who's done more for this country than anyone else I can think of," Toshi whispered, "You wouldn't have heard that speech fifty years ago."

Seeger made his way carefully among the children to the stage. "A long time ago, people didn't *listen* to music," he said. "They *made* music." He asked them to help him sing. "Did any of you ever hear this song?" and he sang, "She'll be wearing red pajamas when she comes—scratch, scratch." When, by the end of the first chorus, no one had sung, he stopped. "Why, I didn't hear you," he said. "Maybe you don't like to sing?" He began playing again and then stopped, as if interrupted by a thought. "Maybe you're *afraid* to sing," he said. Several children widened their eyes. Others stole glances at their teachers. Possibly no grown-up had ever asked them to sing unless it was a hymn or "The Star-Spangled Banner." More often, anyway, one had told them to be quiet.

Seeger said he was going to sing a song he had learned from an Indian. "He said, 'Pete, a lot of our songs are sacred, and it wouldn't be right for a white man to sing them, but here's a canoe song it's all right to sing.'" Pretending to paddle, he chanted, "Kay-oh-wah-chee-nay-o," the syllables falling into the groove of his stroke, so that the song sounded like a work song, or a field holler. When he finished, he began talking about playing a love song, which sounded, he said, like the songs of birds in the woods, and that led him to talk about oyster shells and bone flutes and water birds having lighter bones than other birds, and the bones lending themselves handsomely to making flutes, and then he said, "Oh, let me show you the different sorts of flutes," and he rummaged through a burlap bag he had brought with him that had recorders in it.

"Let's hope he doesn't get lost," Toshi said. "He seldom does."

From the bag, Seeger produced a bass recorder, about as long, a cane. The children murmured at the size. Seeger played "Yankee Doodle Dandy," then he told the children where the song had come from (a British parody of American soldiers sung during the Revolution). "Here's a tune, an Irish tune," he said next. "For three hundred years it had no name, because something very sad had happened. Castle Derry—the English soldiers attacked the castle, and killed all the people in it, so someone made up a melody, and it was so beautiful that people didn't forget it for three hundred years. Then a woman in London gave it a name, 'Londonderry Air.' " He played the song slowly. The children began to clap in an approximate rhythm, and from the side of his mouth, between breaths, and shaking his head, he said emphatically, "No rhythm, no rhythm."

He put down the recorder to sing a spiritual called

"Beyond My Faults." "My voice is not so much any-more," he said when he finished (he thinks that it wobbles and that he might have overused it), "but you get the idea. Anyway, there's time for two or three more songs. I have one you might already know. The fellow who wrote this was a friend of mine. This was sixty-six years ago. He was a little curly-headed guy from Oklahoma who went to California. In California he met another friend of mine who persuaded him to hitchhike east to New York. He was trying to get a job." A girl at Toshi's feet leaned over and put her head in the lap of the girl beside her. Seeger began "This Land Is Your Land," softly and clearly, and the girl sat up and added her voice to everyone else's.

Finally Seeger said, "One more, about a rainbow." He began "Over the Rainbow," then stopped because he had chosen a key that was too high for him. The last line he sang as, "Why, oh why, can't you and I?" In front of Toshi the two girls, holding the final note, with their mouths wide open like bookends, faced each other. The principal returned to the stage and said, "How about a big round of applause for Mr. Seeger, Pete Seeger." He gave Seeger a T-shirt with the school's name on it, a bumper sticker, and a quilt the children had made. Seeger put the shirt on over his own—it said "Soar with Pride, Forrestal Falcons." The children broke ranks and departed for their buses, leaving Seeger alone on the stage, putting his recorders in the burlap bag.

.   .   .

I WENT TO SEE Seeger a few weeks before he turned eighty-nine. It was a Sunday at the end of March, and he was boiling sap over a fire at the end of the yard. The fire was contained in a narrow, three-sided metal stove, a little like a kerosene tank. At one end was an opening with a piece of tin over it, which Seeger would pull aside to feed the fire. Balanced above the flames, slightly below his waist, was a long, shallow, stainless steel tray—a countertop that Seeger had bought from a restaurant-supply house and had inverted to make a pan. Into it, he had poured several gallons of sap as thin and clear as water, until it was about an inch and a half deep. From it rose a sweet-smelling steam. As it cooked, it slowly turned brown. Seeger had notched a chopstick to measure its depth, and when the level reached the lowest notch, he added sap. If the sap got too shallow, it would burn.

When I arrived Seeger was sitting on the grass and feeding logs into the fire. It was a cold, raw day. The river in back of him, reflecting the sky, was the color of tin, or fish scales. With one foot he kicked a log deeper into the fire, then he turned onto his knees and stood. He was wearing jeans and a cloth coat and a knitted wool hat with a pom-pom on it.

I said something about his having lived nearly sixty years in Beacon, and he said, "I never wanted to move. My parents were always moving, and I disapproved of it. Two years here, three years there. Finally, my mother settled down for the last twenty years of her life, in Coral Gables, near Miami. She bought a tiny little house with a tiny little bathroom and a little building in back where she put all her papers, most of which eventually got burned up. When she got to be eighty-nine, she couldn't live by herself anymore and sold the house and moved in with a friend, and didn't know what to do with the papers, and I didn't have time to go through them." He shook his head. "What a loss," he said. "Who knows what was there."

He balled his fists and banged them against his hips, to keep warm. "It's one thing to be a traveling musician," he said, "but I really wanted someplace to move back to, and Toshi loyally provided it. She was talking to herself week after week, month after month. My father only stayed put for his last twelve years. Aunt Elsie, his sister, retired to another tiny little house in Connecticut, and they put a second story on it, and when my father retired about ten years later they lived in it, till she died. He lived another eight or ten years, until he died at age ninety-two. He fell downstairs, whether an accident or a heart attack; they found his body at the bottom of the stairs. When he was ninety, he was getting pessimistic about the world. 'Scientists think that an infinite increase in empirical knowledge is a good thing, but can they prove it,' he would say. He regarded theirs as a religious belief, and a dangerous one."

SEEGER STOOD THE CHOPSTICK in the pan, then poured out another sap bucket. "If I'd had any brains," he said, putting the bucket on the ground, "I'd have taken a year before going to Harvard and studied anthropology at Columbia with Margaret Mead and Franz Boas. I'm absolutely fascinated by anthropology. If we all studied anthropology, we could use it to temper our religion. Alfred North Whitehead, in his essay on the value of education, said, 'A religious education is an education which inculcates duty and reverence.' It *is,* that's what it does. 'And the foundation of reverence is this perception, that the present holds within itself the complete sum of existence, backwards and forwards, that whole amplitude of time, which is eternity.' "

He seemed to entertain that observation, then he sat down in a folding metal chair and spread his hands on his knees. "I'm really kind of dumb now," he said. "I make more mistakes lately than I have in my whole life. My optimism has protected me. And I was blessed with extraordinary good health. I wasn't heavy enough to play regular football, I could compete in track, I liked to pole-vault. Fortunately, I was cautious. I only once tried to climb and nearly killed myself. I climbed trees all the time, though, and took chances I shouldn't. Riding freight trains, I was taking chances. I remember hanging on once by one hand—I had been trying to get on and not managing it properly, and the train was going too fast for me to jump off. I should have been holding on with both hands, but I had the banjo in one hand, and I was thinking, Do I drop the banjo and save myself, or do I try to save both? I didn't have quite the strength, but I made it, with the banjo."

"Did you ever run into trouble on the trains?"

"One time," he said. "In one of the boxcars there were about fifteen or twenty people, and there was a game going on, and in the game was a loudmouth guy, and he was losing all the time. One reason was the other man was cheating on him. Finally the loudmouthed man—who really was objectionable—he bid his watch, and he looked around at the rest of the car and said, 'Anybody want to join this game?' So foolish people around joined in, including me, and he took my last two dollars. Then the car gets to Billings where everybody's getting off to change trains, and between two boxcars I saw the objectionable guy and the guy who had beaten him dividing the spoils, so I said, 'That's what the game is,' and he pulled a knife and said, 'You want to make something of it?' "

Seeger stood up. Over the woodpile was a tarp held down by stones and bricks, and we moved them and rolled back the tarp. The mountains across the river were blue in the hazy light. "Over in those mountains is where Washington turned down the chance to be king of America," Seeger said. "He told them, 'I didn't spend six years fighting royalty to become royalty.' I'm nuts about history, especially New York history." Then he said that below the cliff his house is on there used to be an old house that burned down. "We had a local firebug who went into an institution," he said. "He'd hide in the bushes to watch the excitement. He set kerosene around the house in a ring. I saw it from up here. No one lived in the place. It was a nice mansion, though. Several generations had lived there of a family, and then it had been abandoned." I said something about how still the river looked, and Seeger said, "In August it's like this ninety-nine percent of the time. The sloops could only drift with the tide. It could take weeks to get to Albany, or down to the city."

From beside the stove, Seeger picked up a strainer and dragged it through the sap, removing pieces of leaves and bark. I asked if he had been afraid of going to jail. "At the time my father-in-law was alive, and he wasn't well," he said gravely. He paused, then he said, "I'm an optimist all my life. I felt something would happen, I don't know what, but that I wouldn't go to jail. I probably had too much faith in the Bill of Rights. All my life I've thought what an extraordinary thing the First Amendment is." He shook some froth from the strainer. "What I'm really surprised about is no one's tried to assassinate me up here," he continued. "It would be easy enough to do, and there's people within three miles that would like to do it." He gave a very slight shrug. "I think they didn't because they didn't want to make me famous. You can assassinate Dr. King, but it doesn't make people read his speeches, but I can hear one of them say, 'You kill Seeger, they'll play his songs all over the radio. You'll make him a martyr.' "

He bent over the log pile and stood up a log like a fence post, and leaned one end of it against his chest. He closed his eyes, measuring the weight, then he said, "I think it's too green. I'm going to saw it up for next winter's firewood."

When he had laid down the log, I asked if he saw any pattern to his life.

"I always hated the word *career*," he said. "It implies that fame and fortune are what you're trying to get. I have a life's purpose. In the old days I felt it should be helping the meek to inherit the earth, whether you call the working class the meek or not. Innocently I became a member of the Communist Party, and when they said fight for peace, I did, and when they said fight Hitler, I did. I got out in '49, though, when I moved up here. I should have left much earlier. It was stupid of me not to. My father had got out in '38, when he read the testimony of the trials in Moscow, and he could tell they were forced confessions. We never talked about it, though, and I didn't examine closely enough what was going on. My friends were

mostly Communists, and they said, 'We have to go along with the party.' I didn't realize the danger the world was in; I thought everything would turn out right. I thought Stalin was the brave secretary Stalin, and had no idea how cruel a leader he was."

He began straining the sap again. "These days my purpose is in trying to get people to realize that there may be no human race by the end of the century unless we find ways to talk to people we deeply disagree with," he said. "Whether we cooperate from love or tolerance, it doesn't much matter, but we must treat each other nonviolently. The agricultural revolution took thousands of years, the industrial revolution took hundreds of years, the technological revolution is taking decades. We may just see before much longer the moral revolution which leaders say can come, whether they've been religious leaders, or moral leaders, from Gandhi to Martin Luther King."

A car arrived, driven by the Seegers' grandson, Kitama Jackson, who had come up from the city with two girls and a young man who seemed to know everyone. Kitama is a filmmaker—he had worked on the much admired documentary about Seeger, *The Power of Song,* made by Jim Brown, who had followed Seeger for years—and he set up a video camera on a tripod and began recording his grandfather working at making the syrup. Another of the Seeger grandchildren, Tao Rodriguez-Seeger, a musician who often performs with Seeger, arrived soon after Kitama. Toshi made spoonbread and salad and all of us, including Tinya, Kitama's mother, sat at a table on the deck and ate. Being among a clan is what it felt like. All of them clearly delighted in one another's company. Kitama and Tao conducted most of the conversation, each embroidering the other's stories. Toshi was happier than I had ever seen her.

After the table had been cleared, Tinya drove into the woods and returned with more plastic buckets. The syrup would be done that evening, which was later than I was able to stay. As I walked toward my car, I looked back and saw Seeger standing between Tao and the young man who had come with Kitama.

"Did you really ride boxcars with Woody Guthrie?" the young man asked.

"No, but he taught me how to do it," Seeger said soberly. "You wait outside the station, and when the train's just picking up speed . . ."

A CAMEO, FINALLY, Seeger in relief against the background of himself, courtesy of John Cronin, who is also the director of the Beacon Institute for Rivers and Estuaries: "About two winters ago, here on Route 9 outside Beacon, one winter day it was freezing—rainy and slushy, a miserable winter day—the war in Iraq is heating up, and the country's in a poor mood. I'm driving south, and on the other side of the road I see from the back a tall, slim figure in a hood and coat. I can tell it's Pete. He's standing there all by himself, and he's holding up a big piece of cardboard that clearly has something written on it. Cars and trucks are going by him. He's getting wet. He's holding the homemade sign above his head—he's very tall, and his chin is raised the way he does when he sings—and he's turning the sign in a semicircle, so that the drivers can see it as they pass, and some people are honking and waving at him, and some people are giving him the finger. He's eighty-four years old.

"I know he's got some purpose, of course, but I don't know what it is. What struck me is that, whatever his intentions are, and obviously he wants people to notice what he's doing, he wants to make an impression, anyway, whatever they are, he doesn't call the newspapers and say, 'Here's what I'm going to do, I'm Pete Seeger.' He doesn't cultivate publicity. That isn't what he does. He's far more modest than that. He would never make a fuss. He's just standing out there in the cold and the sleet like a scarecrow getting drenched. I go a little bit down the road, so that I can turn around and come back, and when I get him in view again, this solitary and elderly figure, I see that what he's written on the sign is 'Peace.' "

Appendixes

THE PURPOSES OF MUSIC,
BY CHARLES SEEGER

1. Music, as any art, is not an end in itself, but is a means for achieving larger ends.
2. To *make* music is the essential thing—to listen to it is accessory.
3. Music as a group activity is more important than music as an individual accomplishment.
4. Every person is musical; music can be associated with most human activity, to the advantage of both parties to the association.
5. The musical culture of the nation is, then, to be estimated upon the extent of participation of the whole population rather than upon the extent of the virtuosity of a fraction of it.
6. The basis for the musical culture is the vernacular of the broad mass of the people—its traditional (often called "folk") idiom; popular music and processional music are elaborate superstructures built upon the common base.
7. There is no ground for the quarrel between the various idioms and styles, provided proper relationship between them is maintained—pop need not be scorned nor professional music artificially

stimulated, nor folk music stamped out or sentimentalized.

8. The point of departure for any worker new to a community should be the tastes and capacities actually existent in the group; and the direction of the activities introduced should be more toward the development of local leadership than toward dependence upon outside help.

9. The main question, then, should be not "is it good music?" but "what is music good for?"; and if it bids fair to aid in the welding of the people into more independent, capable and democratic action, it must be approved.

10. With these larger ends ever in view, musicians will frequently find themselves engaged in other kinds of activity, among them the other arts; this, however, promotes a well-rounded social function for them and ensures opportunity to make music serve a well-rounded function in the community.

SEEGER'S TESTIMONY BEFORE THE HOUSE UN-AMERICAN ACTIVITIES COMMITTEE AUGUST 18, 1955

A Subcommittee of the Committee on Un-American Activities met at 10 a.m., in room 1703 of the Federal Building, Foley Square, New York, New York, the Honorable Francis E. Walter (Chairman) presiding.

Committee members present: Representatives Walter, Edwin E. Willis, and Gordon H. Scherer.

Staff members present: Frank S. Tavenner, Jr., Counsel; Donald T. Appell and Frank Bonora, Investigators; and Thomas W. Beale, Sr., Chief Clerk.

MR. TAVENNER: When and where were you born, Mr. Seeger?

MR. SEEGER: I was born in New York in 1919.

MR. TAVENNER: What is your profession or occupation?

MR. SEEGER: Well, I have worked at many things, and my main profession is a student of American folklore, and I make my living as a banjo picker—sort of damning, in some people's opinion.

MR. TAVENNER: Has New York been your headquarters for a considerable period of time?

MR. SEEGER: No, I lived here only rarely until I left school, and after a year or two or a few years living here after World War II I got back to the country, where I always felt more at home.

MR. TAVENNER: You say that you were in the Armed Forces of the United States?

MR. SEEGER: About three and a half years.

MR. TAVENNER: Will you tell us, please, the period of your service?

MR. SEEGER: I went in in July 1942 and I was mustered out in December 1945.

MR. TAVENNER: Did you attain the rank of an officer?

MR. SEEGER: No. After about a year I made Pfc, and just before I got out I got to be T-5, which is the equivalent of a corporal's rating, a long hard pull.

MR. TAVENNER: Mr. Seeger, prior to your entry in the service in 1942, were you engaged in the practice of your profession in the area of New York?

MR. SEEGER: It is hard to call it a profession. I kind of drifted into it and I never intended to be a musician, and I am glad I am one now, and it is a very honorable profession, but when I started out actually I wanted to be a newspaperman, and when I left school—

CHAIRMAN WALTER: Will you answer the question, please?

MR. SEEGER: I have to explain that it really wasn't my profession, I picked up a little change in it.

CHAIRMAN WALTER: Did you practice your profession?

MR. SEEGER: I sang for people, yes, before World War II, and I also did as early as 1925.

MR. TAVENNER: And upon your return from the service in December of 1945, you continued in your profession?

MR. SEEGER: I continued singing, and I expect I always will.

MR. TAVENNER: The Committee has information obtained in part from the *Daily Worker* indicating that, over a period of time, especially since December of 1945, you took part in numerous entertainment features. I have before me a photostatic copy of the June 20, 1947, issue of the *Daily Worker*. In a column entitled "What's On" appears this advertisement: "Tonight–Bronx, hear Peter Seeger and his guitar, at Allerton Section housewarming." May I ask you whether or not the Allerton Section was a section of the Communist Party?

MR. SEEGER: Sir, I refuse to answer that question, whether it was a quote from the *New York Times* or the *Vegetarian Journal*.

MR. TAVENNER: I don't believe there is any more authoritative document in regard to the Communist Party than its official organ, the *Daily Worker*.

MR. SCHERER: He hasn't answered the question, and he merely said he wouldn't answer whether the article appeared in the *New York Times* or some other magazine. I ask you to direct the witness to answer the question.

CHAIRMAN WALTER: I direct you to answer.

MR. SEEGER: Sir, the whole line of questioning—

CHAIRMAN WALTER: You have only been asked one question, so far.

MR. SEEGER: I am not going to answer any questions as to my association, my philosophical or religious beliefs or my political beliefs, or how I voted in any election, or any of these private affairs. I think these are very improper questions for any American to be asked, especially under such compulsion as this. I would be very glad to tell you my life if you want to hear of it.

MR. TAVENNER: Has the witness declined to answer this specific question?

CHAIRMAN WALTER: He said that he is not going to answer any questions, any names or things.

MR. SCHERER: He was directed to answer the question.

MR. TAVENNER: I have before me a photostatic copy of the April 30, 1948, issue of the *Daily Worker,* which carries under the same title of "What's On" an advertisement of a "May Day Rally: For Peace, Security and Democracy." The advertisement states: "Are you in a fighting mood? Then attend the May Day rally." Expert speakers are stated to be slated for the program, and then follows a statement, "Entertainment by Pete Seeger." At the bottom appears this: "Auspices Essex County Communist Party," and at the top, "Tonight, Newark, N.J." Did you lend your talent to the Essex County Communist Party on the occasion indicated by this article from the *Daily Worker*?

MR. SEEGER: Mr. Walter, I believe I have already answered this question, and the same answer.

CHAIRMAN WALTER: The same answer. In other words, you mean that you decline to answer because of the reasons stated before?

MR. SEEGER: I gave my answer, sir.

CHAIRMAN WALTER: What is your answer?

MR. SEEGER: You see, sir, I feel—

CHAIRMAN WALTER: What is your answer?

MR. SEEGER: I will tell you what my answer is.

(Witness consulted with counsel [Paul L. Ross].)

I feel that in my whole life I have never done anything of any conspiratorial nature, and I resent very much and very deeply the implication of being called before this Committee that in some way because my opinions may be different from yours, or yours, Mr. Willis, or yours, Mr. Scherer, that I am any less of an American than anybody else. I love my country very deeply, sir.

CHAIRMAN WALTER: Why don't you make a little contribution toward preserving its institutions?

MR. SEEGER: I feel that my whole life is a contribution. That is why I would like to tell you about it.

The Protest Singer

CHAIRMAN WALTER: I don't want to hear about it.

MR. SCHERER: I think that there must be a direction to answer.

CHAIRMAN WALTER: I direct you to answer that question.

MR. SEEGER: I have already given you my answer, sir.

MR. SCHERER: Let me understand. You are not relying on the Fifth Amendment, are you?

MR. SEEGER: No, sir, although I do not want to in any way discredit or depreciate or deprecate the witnesses that have used the Fifth Amendment, and I simply feel it is improper for this Committee to ask such questions.

MR. SCHERER: And then in answering the rest of the questions, or in refusing to answer the rest of the questions, I understand that you are not relying on the Fifth Amendment as a basis for your refusal to answer?

MR. SEEGER: No, I am not, sir.

MR. TAVENNER: I have before me a photostatic copy of the May 4, 1949, issue of the *Daily Worker,* which has an article entitled, "May Day Smash Review Put On by Communist Cultural Division, On Stage," and the article was written by Bob Reed. This article emphasizes a production called *Now Is the Time,* and it says this: *Now Is the Time* was a hard-hitting May Day show of songs and knife-edged satire. New songs and film strips walloped the enemies of the people in what the singers called

"Aesopian language." And other persons [participated], including Pete Seeger. Lee Hays is recited to be the MC, or master of ceremonies. Did you take part in this May Day program under the auspices of the Music Section of the Cultural Division of the Communist Party?

MR. SEEGER: Mr. Chairman, the answer is the same as before.

MR. SCHERER: I think we have to have a direction.

CHAIRMAN WALTER: I direct you to answer the question.

MR. SEEGER: I have given you my answer, sir.

MR. TAVENNER: The article contains another paragraph, as follows: This performance of *Now Is the Time* was given in honor of the twelve indicted Communist Party leaders. And then it continues with Bob Reed's account of the show: This reviewer has never seen a show which stirred its audience more. Add up new material, fine personal and group performances, overwhelming audience response—the result was a significant advance in the people's cultural movement. *Now Is the Time* is that rare phenomenon, a political show in which performers and audience had a lot of fun. It should be repeated for large audiences. Mr. Lee Hays was asked, while he was on the witness stand, whether or not he wrote that play, and he refused to answer. Do you know whether he was the originator of the script?

MR. SEEGER: Do I know whether he was the originator of the script? Again my answer is the same.
However, if you want to question me about any
songs, I would be glad to tell you, sir.

CHAIRMAN WALTER: That is what you are being
asked about now.

MR. TAVENNER: You said that you would tell us about
the songs. Did you participate in a program at
Wingdale Lodge in the State of New York, which is
a summer camp for adults and children, on the
weekend of July Fourth of this year?
(Witness consulted with counsel.)

MR. SEEGER: Again, I say I will be glad to tell what
songs I have ever sung, because singing is my
business.

MR. TAVENNER: I am going to ask you.

MR. SEEGER: But I decline to say who has ever listened to them, who has written them, or other people who have sung them.

MR. TAVENNER: Did you sing this song, to which we
have referred, "Now Is the Time," at Wingdale
Lodge on the weekend of July Fourth?

MR. SEEGER: I don't know any song by that name,
and I know a song with a similar name. It is called
"Wasn't That a Time." Is that the song?

CHAIRMAN WALTER: Did you sing that song?

MR. SEEGER: I can sing it. I don't know how well I can
do it without my banjo.

CHAIRMAN WALTER: I said, Did you sing it on that occasion?

MR. SEEGER: I have sung that song. I am not going to go into where I have sung it. I have sung it many places.

CHAIRMAN WALTER: Did you sing it on this particular occasion? That is what you are being asked.

MR. SEEGER: Again my answer is the same.

CHAIRMAN WALTER: You said that you would tell us about it.

MR. SEEGER: I will tell you about the songs, but I am not going to tell you or try to explain—

CHAIRMAN WALTER: I direct you to answer the question. Did you sing this particular song on the Fourth of July at Wingdale Lodge in New York?

MR. SEEGER: I have already given you my answer to that question, and all questions such as that. I feel that is improper: to ask about my associations and opinions. I have said that I would be voluntarily glad to tell you any song, or what I have done in my life.

CHAIRMAN WALTER: I think it is my duty to inform you that we don't accept this answer and the others, and I give you an opportunity now to answer these questions, particularly the last one.

MR. SEEGER: Sir, my answer is always the same.

CHAIRMAN WALTER: All right, go ahead, Mr. Tavenner.

MR. TAVENNER: Were you chosen by Mr. Elliott Sullivan to take part in the program on the weekend of July Fourth at Wingdale Lodge?

MR. SEEGER: The answer is the same, sir.

MR. WILLIS: Was that the occasion of the satire on the Constitution and the Bill of Rights?

MR. TAVENNER: The same occasion, yes, sir. I have before me a photostatic copy of a page from the June 1, 1949, issue of the *Daily Worker,* and in a column entitled "Town Talk" there is found this statement: The first performance of a new song, "If I Had a Hammer," on the theme of the Foley Square trial of the Communist leaders, will be given at a testimonial dinner for the twelve on Friday night at St. Nicholas Arena. . . . Among those on hand for the singing will be . . . Pete Seeger, and Lee Hays—and others whose names are mentioned. Did you take part in that performance?

MR. SEEGER: I shall be glad to answer about the song, sir, and I am not interested in carrying on the line of questioning about where I have sung any songs.

MR. TAVENNER: I ask a direction.

CHAIRMAN WALTER: You may not be interested, but we are, however. I direct you to answer. You can answer that question.

MR. SEEGER: I feel these questions are improper, sir, and I feel they are immoral to ask any American this kind of question.

MR. TAVENNER: Have you finished your answer?

MR. SEEGER: Yes, sir.

MR. TAVENNER: I desire to offer the document in evidence and ask that it be marked "Seeger exhibit no. 4," for identification only, and to be made a part of the Committee files.

MR. SEEGER: I am sorry you are not interested in the song. It is a good song.

MR. TAVENNER: Were you present in the hearing room while the former witnesses testified?

MR. SEEGER: I have been here all morning, yes, sir.

MR. TAVENNER: I assume then that you heard me read the testimony of Mr. [Elia] Kazan about the purpose of the Communist Party in having its actors entertain for the benefit of Communist fronts and the Communist Party. Did you hear that testimony?

MR. SEEGER: Yes, I have heard all of the testimony today.

MR. TAVENNER: Did you hear Mr. George Hall's testimony yesterday in which he stated that, as an actor, the special contribution that he was expected to make to the Communist Party was to use his talents by entertaining at Communist Party functions? Did you hear that testimony?

MR. SEEGER: I didn't hear it, no.

MR. TAVENNER: It is a fact that he so testified. I want to know whether or not you were engaged in a similar type of service to the Communist Party in entertaining at these features.

(Witness consulted with counsel.)

MR. SEEGER: I have sung for Americans of every political persuasion, and I am proud that I never refuse to sing to an audience, no matter what religion or color of their skin, or situation in life. I have sung in hobo jungles, and I have sung for the Rockefellers, and I am proud that I have never refused to sing for anybody. That is the only answer I can give along that line.

CHAIRMAN WALTER: Mr. Tavenner, are you getting around to that letter? There was a letter introduced yesterday that I think was of greater importance than any bit of evidence adduced at these hearings, concerning the attempt made to influence people in this professional performers' guild and union to assist a purely Communist cause which had no relation whatsoever to the arts and the theater. Is that what you are leading up to?

MR. TAVENNER: Yes, it is. That was the letter of Peter Lawrence, which I questioned him about yesterday. That related to the trial of the Smith Act defendants here at Foley Square. I am trying to inquire now whether this witness was party to the same type of propaganda effort by the Communist Party.

MR. SCHERER: There has been no answer to your last question.

MR. TAVENNER: That is right; may I have a direction?

MR. SEEGER: Would you repeat the question? I don't even know what the last question was, and I thought I have answered all of them up to now.

MR. TAVENNER: What you stated was not in response to the question.

CHAIRMAN WALTER: Proceed with the questioning, Mr. Tavenner.

MR. TAVENNER: I believe, Mr. Chairman, with your permission, I will have the question read to him. I think it should be put in exactly the same form.

(Whereupon the reporter read the pending question as above recorded.)

MR. SEEGER: "These features": What do you mean? Except for the answer I have already given you, I have no answer. The answer I gave you you have, don't you? That is, that I am proud that I have sung for Americans of every political persuasion, and I have never refused to sing for anybody because I disagreed with their political opinion, and I am proud of the fact that my songs seem to cut across and find perhaps a unifying thing, basic humanity, and that is why I would love to be able to tell you about these songs, because I feel that you would agree with me more, sir. I know many beautiful songs from your home county, Carbon, and Monroe, and I hitchhiked through there and stayed in the homes of miners.

MR. TAVENNER: My question was whether or not you sang at these functions of the Communist Party.

You have answered it inferentially, and if I understand your answer, you are saying you did.

MR. SEEGER: Except for that answer, I decline to answer further.

MR. TAVENNER: Did you sing at functions of the Communist Party, at Communist Party requests?

MR. SEEGER: I believe, sir, that a good twenty minutes ago, I gave my answer to this whole line of questioning.

MR. TAVENNER: Yes, but you have now beclouded your answer by your statement, and I want to make certain what you mean. Did you sing at the Communist Party functions which I have asked you about, as a Communist Party duty?

MR. SEEGER: I have already indicated that I am not interested, and I feel it is improper to say who has sung my songs or who I have sung them to, especially under such compulsion as this.

MR. TAVENNER: Have you been a member of the Communist Party since 1947?

(Witness consulted with counsel.)

MR. SEEGER: The same answer, sir.

CHAIRMAN WALTER: I direct you to answer that question.

MR. SEEGER: I must give the same answer as before.

MR. TAVENNER: I have a throwaway sheet entitled "Culture Fights Back, 1953," showing entertainment at the Capitol Hotel, Carnival Room, Fifty-first Street at Eighth Avenue, in 1953, sponsored by the Committee to Defend V. J. Jerome. It indicates that Pete Seeger was one of those furnishing the entertainment. Will you tell the Committee, please, whether or not you were asked to perform on that occasion, and whether or not you did, either as a Communist Party directive, or as what you considered to be a duty to the Communist Party?

MR. SEEGER: I believe I have answered this already.

MR. TAVENNER: Are you acquainted with V. J. Jerome?

MR. SEEGER: I have already told you, sir, that I believe my associations, whatever they are, are my own private affairs.

MR. TAVENNER: You did know, at that time, in 1953, that V. J. Jerome was a cultural head of the Communist Party and one of the Smith Act defendants in New York City?

MR. SEEGER: Again the same answer, sir.

MR. SCHERER: You refuse to answer that question?

MR. SEEGER: Yes, sir.

MR. TAVENNER: I hand you a photograph which was taken of the May Day parade in New York City in 1952, which shows the front rank of a group of individuals, and one is in a uniform with military cap and insignia, and carrying a placard entitled CENSORED. Will you examine it, please, and state whether or not that is a photograph of you?

(A document was handed to the witness.)

MR. SEEGER: It is like Jesus Christ when asked by Pontius Pilate, "Are you king of the Jews?"

CHAIRMAN WALTER: Stop that.

MR. SEEGER: Let someone else identify that picture.

MR. SCHERER: I ask that he be directed to answer the question.

CHAIRMAN WALTER: I direct you to answer the question.

MR. SEEGER: Do I identify this photograph?

CHAIRMAN WALTER: Yes.

MR. SEEGER: I say let someone else identify it.

MR. TAVENNER: I desire to offer the document in evidence and ask that it be marked "Seeger exhibit no. 6."

CHAIRMAN WALTER: Make it a part of the record.

(Witness consulted with counsel.)

MR. TAVENNER: It is noted that the individual mentioned is wearing a military uniform. That was in May of 1952, and the statute of limitations would have run by now as to any offense for the improper wearing of the uniform, and will you tell the Committee whether or not you took part in that May Day program wearing a uniform of an American soldier?

MR. SEEGER: The same answer as before, sir.

CHAIRMAN WALTER: I direct you to answer that question.

(Witness consulted with counsel.)

MR. SCHERER: I think the record should show that the witness remains mute, following the direction by the Chairman to answer that question.

MR. SEEGER: The same answer, sir, as before.

MR. SCHERER: Again, I understand that you are not invoking the Fifth Amendment?

MR. SEEGER: That is correct.

MR. SCHERER: We are not accepting the answers or the reasons you gave.

MR. SEEGER: That is your prerogative, sir.

MR. SCHERER: Do you understand it is the feeling of the Committee that you are in contempt as a result of the position you take?

MR. SEEGER: I can't say.

MR. SCHERER: I am telling you that that is the position of the Committee.

MR. TAVENNER: The *Daily Worker* of April 21, 1948, at page 7, contains a notice that Pete Seeger was a participant in an affair for Ferdinand Smith. Will you tell the Committee what the occasion was at which you took part?

MR. SEEGER: I hate to waste the Committee's time, but I think surely you must realize by now that my answer is the same.

MR. TAVENNER: Do you know whether Ferdinand Smith was under deportation orders at that time?

MR. SEEGER: My answer is the same as before, sir.

MR. TAVENNER: I think that he was not under deportation orders until a little later than that.

CHAIRMAN WALTER: What is his name?

MR. TAVENNER: Ferdinand Smith, a Communist Party member and former vice-president of the maritime union. My purpose in asking you these questions, Mr. Seeger, is to determine whether or not, in accordance with the plan of the Communist Party as outlined by Mr. Kazan and Mr. George Hall, you were performing a valuable service to the Communist Party, and if that was the way they attempted to use you.

MR. SEEGER: Is that a question, sir?

MR. TAVENNER: That is my explanation to you, with the hope that you will give the Committee some light on that subject.

MR. SEEGER: No, my answer is the same as before.

MR. TAVENNER: Did you also perform and entertain at various functions held by front organizations, such as the American Youth for Democracy? I have here photostatic copies of the *Daily Worker* indicating such programs were conducted in Detroit in 1952, at Greenwich Village on May 10, 1947, and again at another place in March of 1948. Did you entertain at functions under the auspices of the American Youth for Democracy?

(Witness consulted with counsel.)

MR. SEEGER: The answer is the same, and I take it that you are not interested in all of the different places that I have sung. Why don't you ask me about the churches and schools and other places?

MR. TAVENNER: That is very laudable, indeed, and I wish only that your activities had been confined to those areas. If you were acting for the Communist Party at these functions, we want to know it. We want to determine just what the Communist Party plan was.

MR. SCHERER: Witness, you have indicated that you are perfectly willing to tell us about all of these innumerable functions at which you entertained, but why do you refuse to tell us about the functions that Mr. Tavenner inquires about?

MR. SEEGER: No, sir, I said that I should be glad to tell you about all of the songs that I have sung, because I feel that the songs are the clearest explanation of what I do believe in, as a musician, and as an American.

MR. SCHERER: Didn't you just say that you sang before various religious groups, school groups?

MR. SEEGER: I have said it and I will say it again, and I have sung for perhaps—

(Witness consulted with counsel.)

MR. SCHERER: You are willing to tell us about those groups?

MR. SEEGER: I am saying voluntarily that I have sung for almost every religious group in the country, from Jewish and Catholic, and Presbyterian and Holy Rollers and Revival Churches, and I do this voluntarily. I have sung for many, many different groups—and it is hard for perhaps one person to believe, I was looking back over the twenty years or so that I have sung around these forty-eight states, that I have sung in so many different places.

MR. SCHERER: Did you sing before the groups that Mr. Tavenner asked you about?

MR. SEEGER: I am saying that my answer is the same as before. I have told you that I sang for everybody.

CHAIRMAN WALTER: Wait a minute. You sang for everybody. Then are we to believe, or to take it, that you sang at the places Mr. Tavenner mentioned?

MR. SEEGER: My answer is the same as before.

CHAIRMAN WALTER: What is that?

MR. SEEGER: It seems to me like the third time I have said it, if not the fourth.

CHAIRMAN WALTER: Maybe it is the fifth, but say it again. I want to know what your answer is.

(Witness consulted with counsel.)

MR. SEEGER: I decline to discuss, under compulsion, where I have sung, and who has sung my songs, and who else has sung with me, and the people I have known. I love my country very dearly, and I greatly resent this implication that some of the places that I have sung and some of the people that I have known, and some of my opinions, whether they are religious or philosophical, or I might be a vegetarian, make me any less of an American. I will tell you about my songs, but I am not interested in telling you who wrote them, and I will tell you about my songs, and I am not interested in who listened to them.

MR. TAVENNER: According to the *Daily Worker,* there was a conference program of the Civil Rights Congress on April 2, 1949, at which you were one of the performers. On August 27, 1949, the People's Artists presented a summer musicale at Lakeland Acres picnic grounds, Peekskill, New York, for the benefit of the Harlem chapter of the Civil Rights Congress, at which you were a participant. At another meeting of the Civil Rights Congress of New York, around May 11, 1946, you were a participant. Will you tell the Committee, please, under what circumstances you performed, because you have said that you sang at all sorts of meetings. Under what circumstances were your services acquired on those occasions?

MR. SEEGER: My answer is the same as before, sir. I can only infer from your lack of interest in my songs that you are actually scared to know what these songs are like, because there is nothing wrong with my songs, sir. Do you know—

MR. SCHERER: You said you want to talk about your songs, and I will give you an opportunity. Tell us what songs you sang at Communist Party meetings?

MR. SEEGER: I will tell you about the songs that I have sung any place.

MR. SCHERER: I want to know the ones that you sang at Communist Party meetings, because those are the songs about which we can inquire. Just tell us one song that you sang at a Communist Party meeting.

MR. SEEGER: Mr. Scherer, it seems to me that you heard my testimony, and that is a ridiculous question, because you know what my answer is.

MR. TAVENNER: Mr. George Hall testified that the entertainment that he engaged in, at the insistence of the Communist Party, was not songs of a political character. He did say, however, that he was expected by the Communist Party to perform in order to raise money for the Communist Party. Now, did you, as Mr. Hall did, perform in order to raise money for Communist Party causes?

(Witness consulted with counsel.)

MR. SEEGER: I don't care what Mr. Hall says, and my answer is the same as before, sir.

MR. TAVENNER: That you refuse to answer?

MR. SEEGER: I have given my answer.

MR. SCHERER: Was Mr. Hall telling the truth when he told the Committee about the entertainment he engaged in at the insistence of the Communist Party?

MR. SEEGER: I don't feel like discussing what Mr. Hall said.

MR. TAVENNER: The American Committee for Yugoslav Relief has been designated as a front organization. According to the October 22, 1947, issue of the *Daily People's World,* in California, Pete Seeger headed the list of entertainers to appear at a picnic given by the Southern California chapter of that organization. Did you participate in that program?

MR. SEEGER: If you have a hundred more photostats there, it seems silly for me to give you the same answer a hundred more times.

MR. TAVENNER: What is your answer?

MR. SEEGER: It is the same as before, sir.

MR. TAVENNER: There are various peace groups in the country which have utilized your services, are there not?

MR. SEEGER: I have sung for pacifists and I have sung for soldiers.

MR. TAVENNER: According to the *Daily Worker* of September 6, 1940, you were scheduled as a singer at a mass meeting of the American Peace Mobilization at Turner's Arena, in Washington, D.C. What were the circumstances under which you were requested to take part in that performance?

MR. SEEGER: My answer is the same as before, sir.

MR. TAVENNER: You were a member of the American Peace Mobilization, were you not?

MR. SEEGER: My answer is the same as before.

MR. TAVENNER: Were you not a delegate to the Chicago convention of the American Peace Mobilization on September 5, 1940?

MR. SEEGER: My answer is the same as before.

CHAIRMAN WALTER: Is that organization subversive?

MR. TAVENNER: Yes.

CHAIRMAN WALTER: What is the name of it?

MR. TAVENNER: American Peace Mobilization, and it was the beginning of these peace organizations, back in 1940. Did you take part in the American Peace Crusade program in Chicago in April of 1954?

MR. SEEGER: My answer is the same as before. Of course, I would be curious to know what you think of a song like this very great Negro spiritual, "I'm Gonna Lay Down My Sword and Shield, Down by the Riverside."

MR. TAVENNER: That is not at all responsive to my question.

MR. SEEGER: I gave you my answer before I even said that.

MR. TAVENNER: If you refuse to answer, I think that you should not make a speech.

(Witness consulted with counsel.)

MR. TAVENNER: Did you also perform a service for the California Labor School in Los Angeles by putting on musical programs there?

MR. SEEGER: My answer is the same as before, sir.

MR. TAVENNER: Did you teach in the California Labor School?

MR. SEEGER: My answer is the same as before, sir.

MR. SCHERER: I think for the record you should state

whether the California Labor School has been cited.

MR. TAVENNER: It has.

MR. SCHERER: As subversive and Communist dominated?

MR. TAVENNER: Yes, it has been.

(Witness consulted with counsel.)

MR. TAVENNER: Did you also teach at the Jefferson School of Social Science here in the city of New York?

MR. SEEGER: My answer is the same as before, sir.

MR. SCHERER: I ask that you direct him to answer.

CHAIRMAN WALTER: I direct you to answer. Did you teach at the Jefferson School here at New York?

MR. SEEGER: I feel very silly having to repeat the same thing over and over again, but my answer is exactly the same as before, sir.

CHAIRMAN WALTER: Has the Jefferson School of Social Science been cited?

MR. TAVENNER: Yes, and it has been required to register under the 1950 Internal Security Act.

MR. SCHERER: There are a number of people here who taught at that school, Mr. Walter.

MR. TAVENNER: I desire to offer in evidence a photostatic copy of an article from the September 21, 1946, issue of the *Daily Worker* which refers to music courses at Jefferson School, and I call attention to the last sentence in the article wherein Peter Seeger is mentioned as a leader in one of the courses. * * *

According to the March 18, 1948, issue of the *Daily Worker,* it is indicated that you would entertain at a musical presented by the Jefferson Workers' Bookshop. According to the November 25, 1948, issue of the same paper you would perform also under the auspices of the Jefferson School of Social Science. Also you were a participant in a program advertised in the *Daily Worker* of June 1, 1950, put on by the Jefferson School of Social Science, and according to an issue of February 15, 1954, of the same paper, you were expected to play and lecture on songs and ballads in the Jefferson School. Will you tell the Committee, please, what were the circumstances under which you engaged in those programs, if you did?

MR. SEEGER: My answer is the same as before, sir.

MR. TAVENNER: Did you also engage in performances for the Labor Youth League in 1954?

MR. SEEGER: My answer is the same as before. Did you think that I sing propaganda songs or something?

MR. TAVENNER: In 1947, what was your connection with an organization known as People's Songs?
(Witness consulted with counsel.)

MR. SEEGER: I take the same answer as before regarding any organization or any association I have.

CHAIRMAN WALTER: What was People's Songs, Mr. Tavenner?

MR. TAVENNER: People's Songs was an organization

which, according to its issue of February and March 1947, was composed of a number of persons on the board of directors who have been called before this Committee or identified by this Committee as members of the Communist Party, and the purpose of which, from information made available to the Committee, was to extend services to the Communist Party in its entertainment projects. Mr. Lee Hays was a member of the board of directors, was he not, along with you, in this organization?

(Witness consulted with counsel.)

MR. SEEGER: My answer is the same as before, sir.

MR. TAVENNER: Were you not the editor of People's Songs, and a member of the board of directors in 1947?

MR. SEEGER: My answer is the same as before.

MR. TAVENNER: You were actually the national director of this organization, were you not?

MR. SEEGER: My answer is the same as before.

MR. TAVENNER: Was the organization founded by Alan Lomax?

MR. SEEGER: My answer is the same as before.

MR. TAVENNER: Was the booking agent of People's Songs an organization known as People's Artists?

MR. SEEGER: My answer is the same.

MR. TAVENNER: Will you tell the Committee, please, whether or not during the weekend of July 4, 1955, you were a member of the Communist Party?

MR. SEEGER: My answer is the same as before, sir.

MR. TAVENNER: Were you a member of the Communist Party at any time during the various entertainment features in which you were alleged to have engaged?

MR. SEEGER: My answer is the same.

MR. TAVENNER: Are you a member of the Communist Party now?

MR. SEEGER: My answer is the same.

MR. SCHERER: I ask for a direction on that question.

CHAIRMAN WALTER: I direct you to answer.

MR. SEEGER: My answer is the same as before.

MR. TAVENNER: I have no further questions, Mr. Chairman.

CHAIRMAN WALTER: The witness is excused.

ACKNOWLEDGMENTS

In addition to the people whose names appear in the text, I would like above all to thank David Remnick, who first suggested that I write about Seeger. Also Dana Goodyear, Virginia Cannon, and Amy Davidson; Ann Close, Marty Asher, and Caroline Zancan; Andrew Wylie, Jin Auh, and Jacqueline Ko; Garrison Keillor, Mike Seeger, and Joan Baez; Kate and Brookie Maxwell; Leland, Kirk, and Stephan Wilkinson; Ry Cooder and Bob Weir.

Sara Barrett suggested that the book have photographs and then worked tirelessly to find and arrange them so handsomely.

ILLUSTRATIONS

the easel behind her. Seeger does not recall ever seeing the painting.

PHOTOGRAPHIC CREDITS

All photographs courtesy of Pete and Toshi Seeger except:

PAGE 7 Jim Marshall
11 Erik Falkensteen
15 David Gahr
18 Jim Marshall
20 Sara Barrett
31 Museum of the City of New York
58 The Woody Guthrie Archives
72 Getty Images
77 Corbis
92 Take Stock Photos
99 Getty Images
103 Keith Meyers / *The New York Times*
117 Getty Images

A NOTE ABOUT THE AUTHOR

Alec Wilkinson began writing for *The New Yorker* in 1980. Before that, he was a policeman in Wellfleet, Massachusetts, and before that he was a rock-and-roll musician. He has published eight other books—two memoirs, two collections of essays, two biographical portraits, and two pieces of reporting. His honors include a Guggenheim Fellowship, a Lyndhurst Prize, and a Robert F. Kennedy Book Award. He lives with his wife and son in New York City.

A NOTE ON THE TYPE

This book was set in a type called Baskerville. The face itself is a facsimile reproduction of types cast from the molds made for John Baskerville (1706–1775) from his designs. Baskerville's original face was one of the forerunners of the type style known to printers as "modern face"–a "modern" of the period A.D. 1800.

COMPOSED BY

North Market Street Graphics, Lancaster, Pennsylvania

PRINTED AND BOUND BY

RRD Harrisonburg, Harrisonburg, Virginia

DESIGNED BY

Iris Weinstein